The Giant Killers

TAKING ON AMERICA'S LARGEST CORPORATIONS

D1285952

Published by Titan Publishing
ISBN 978-1-4392-7409-5
Library of Congress Number 2010911803

Printed in the United States of America by
CreateSpace, a part of the Amazon Group of Companies.

To Larry —
Finally done!
Thanks for your
help —

Best regards —
Bob Parent
Jan 2011

The Giant Killers

TAKING ON AMERICA'S LARGEST CORPORATIONS

Contents

FOREWORD

Bob - what a run! What a remarkable journey! You have been there; you had done it.

Now you are sharing it with all of us in this great book of yours. What great revelations; a military experience that took you to Europe during World War II; a good marriage and a family life that has expanded over fifty-five years; the second love of your life, "the law," and now an Author.

This book is such easy reading and interesting, making one feel as though he or she is traveling with Bob when he tells you about his successful law practice in Michigan around the Pontiac and Detroit areas. Finally, he takes us to the time when he decided he would retire and move his family to South Florida on the water where he used his boat to fish and travel to the Bahamas. This retirement was short lived after he met up with a young fiery Black lawyer named Willie Gary, who later became known as the "giant killer." Willie, along with his partner, Lorenzo Williams, convinced Bob that he was too young to retire and invited him to join forces with them in their law firm. Until today, I do not know how this union was ever formed because both Willie and Bob are competitive and egotistical lawyers, and loosing was never an option to either.

Bob never stood for the status quo. Bob always subscribed to the philosophy of Ed Bradley, "Be prepared, work hard, and hope for a little good luck. Recognize that the harder you work and the better prepared you are, the more luck you might have." His story in this book is a historical part of the transformation in the legal system where hard work and good preparation for trial, transcend the prejudices and stereotypes that pervaded in the legal system in the Deep South when he teamed up with the "giant killer," Willie Gary, who was successfully rising in the area of personal injury. The firm later extended their expertise into the area of commercial litigation, taking on the big corporations of America like Disney, Anheuser-Busch, Motorola and Loewen Group, and being successful in each one they took on as defendants. The memoirs in this book share some of Bob's most gratifying experiences while practicing law as the only white attorney in a three-man African American law firm that graduated into becoming a law firm in excess of 150 members, including support staff. This law firm is a premier trial firm, which is among the finest trial law firms in America, and in this book, Bob shares how they sued and prevailed against some of the biggest corporations in America who were represented by some of the most prestigious law firms in America.

It is so strange how I first met Bob and developed an everlasting friendship with him. We met as adversaries in the court arena while he was representing a female client in a divorce proceeding. The husband retained me after he had been incarcerated for contempt of court for failure to pay Bob's client child support. Bob and I entered into a stipulation which permitted my client to purge himself on the contempt order by making partial increment payments toward the arrearages support money and Bob agreed to have my client released from incarceration. From the onset of this experience, Bob and I became good professional friends and we there afterward associated on many cases together. The female client whom he represented in the divorce became one of my secretaries and worked for me until her untimely demise.

Thanks, Bob, for writing such an entertaining book that shares with the readers your love of family, love of country through your military service, and for your many commitments as a lawyer. You have worked unselfishly in excess of fifty-five years protecting the rights and freedom of your clients, and all citizens of this great country; all for which we thank you.

T.J. Cunningham, Sr., Esq.
Senior Partner of Cunningham & Cunningham, P.A.
Serving South Florida for over fifty years

PREFACE

This book is a sequel to my first publication, *A Story of Love and War*, based on my true-life experiences in World War II, and my life upon returning to civilian life from the battlefields of Europe; after which time, I married Laurie, my USO sweetheart, completed law school on the GI Bill and raised a family.

At the end of a successful legal career, I commenced another by teaming up with powerhouse trial lawyer, Willie E. Gary, in Stuart, Florida. As you will read in the pages to follow, our battles together brought corporate America to its knees in nationally known, high profile cases against Loewen - a Canadian funeral home conglomerate, Disney Company, Budweiser and Motorola.

This book is based on those true courtroom experiences that pit the country's finest trial lawyers against each other in gladiatorial combat, where the outcome could well determine the future success or failure of professional careers.

In writing this book, I hope to share these experiences with you, and provide fascinating insight into "behind the scenes" strategy and courtroom drama that led to unprecedented victories against tenacious foes, financed by unlimited resources.

I also provide my perspective on the contingency fee agreement between client and lawyer, and the role it plays in making legal services available to all citizens who seek a key to the courtroom door and justice in America.

ACKNOWLEDGMENTS

Without the endeavors of the cadre that stand behind the scenes enabling the courtroom lawyers to perform their act in the theater of justice, this story could never have been told. They rarely receive the credit they deserve for participating in the conduct of trials that are occurring every day in our country's halls of justice.

My wife Laurie was my "home" secretary. She did most of the typing and computer transcriptions and sat through many days of trial in almost every case. She provided help and support when I needed it, as did our children - Rob, Dave and Christine. Special thanks and love go to them for putting up with me "through the years."

My office secretary of over twenty years, Mickey Wright, was involved in every case recited here, and probably has greater knowledge of the details of those cases than anyone else involved.

In recognition and gratitude to the excellent lawyers that assisted during the trials and encouraged me in the publication of this work, I express my gratitude. In addition to those mentioned during the narrative, those include Manuel Socias, C.K. Hoffler, Maria Sperando, Jean Laws Scott, Mary Ann Diaz, Arnold Gaines, Debra Nolan, Paul Finizio, Jamie Finizio Bascomb, Charlene Banks and Bruce Rogow; the able paralegals involved must be mentioned, including Mel Wrice, Joey Zaratan, Kerry Hyde and Chris Nannini. In addition, Steve Hedrick and Kelvin McMiller of the support staff were always there to respond when travel help was needed. Often overlooked in the contributions by staff include our computer people, Kevin Mulligan and Mike Conklin.

Particular thanks must go to Jason Brodie, our graphic artist and computer expert, who was instrumental in putting the book together in digital form, designing the cover and associating with the publisher. This work could never have been completed without his help. Additionally, I express my gratitude to Melissa Cleveland, who put the "final polish" on this book as the editor. I appreciate her patience in making corrections and her suggestions in the final stages of this book.

I was fortunate to have personal friend, Kim Vought, Esq., a "Silk Stocking" Philadelphia trial lawyer, now retired, offer insight and perspective from the defense. His astute observations from the other side of the courtroom were indeed helpful in tempering some of my opinion. Attorney T.J. Cunningham provided historical background of the educational barriers facing early black aspirants to the Florida Bar.

Joan Howarth, dean of the School of Law at Michigan State University, provided invaluable editing suggestions and professorial assistance as did Ike Crumpler, journalist and media consultant. Lawrence T. (Larry) Sullivan, now retired, associate editor of the Detroit News for many years, offered invaluable assistance, suggestions and historical background of the city of Detroit's tumultuous events during the post war years. Their continued encouragement renewed my times of abating energy. Writing reality is not easy, especially for a lawyer.

To those that participated, but unintentionally not mentioned here, your assistance in contributing to the worth of this work is appreciated.

I

LAWYERS - JUDGES - JURIES

I consider trial by jury as the only anchor ever yet imagined
by man, by which a government can be held to the
principles of its constitution.
THOMAS JEFFERSON, letter to Thomas Paine (1789)

Enraged wives take their husbands to task for dallying with secretaries. Murderers and rapists are punished for their vile deeds. Children battle over their parents' wealth. Injured people demand recompense from those who hurt them. Cavemen settled these disputes with clubs and stones; survival of the fittest. As humans became more civilized, alternate means of settling their problems evolved. Those with the resources hired somebody else to fight their battles for them; survival of the wealthiest. So it has been since the emergence of that which we call civilization.

Just as medieval knights and ancient samurai settled their sponsors' disputes, American lawyers are called into battle whenever people disagree. Their battlefields are courtrooms, where the results often produce lost dreams, broken lives and financial ruin. We call it justice.

Is the American system of justice out of hand? Or is the society it tries to serve out of hand? The system is being asked each day to solve the problems created by ordinary people leading ordinary lives in an ordinary world where people differ little from their ancestors; however, in America the stakes are higher than ever before. People have much more to win or lose. Prosperity is the product of greed and never has history witnessed a more prosperous or greedier society than modern America.

To say that Americans are litigious simply states the obvious. Americans are greedy. Offended wives want revenge, but most will settle for their husband's entire fortune. Vicious criminals want their freedom, but will settle for the shortest prison sentence possible, only to be set loose to once again prey on their neighbors. The family of a man killed by a drunken driver wants the culprit punished, but usually will exchange that retribution for the right amount of cash.

Americans also worship winning. Most do not have the wherewithal - financial, physical or intellectual, to ascend life's ladder to the top. Few get past the first couple of rungs. For this pronounced majority, the wheel of fortune is a lottery or a lawsuit. The odds of winning a lawsuit are better, but not much. The vast majority of lawsuits, estimated at over 95 percent, never get to trial. They are settled or thrown out. Still, the system is overworked, understaffed and ill prepared to deal with the massive volume of complaints brought to halls of justice each day across America.

Unsophisticated individuals are not alone in their pursuit of greed and avarice. Their foolishness pales in light of the corporate executives who so selfishly guard their paychecks and fringe benefits by shamelessly employing any means available to keep their companies profitable or to please superiors.

Consider Ford Motor Company's decision regarding the Pinto automobile during the 1970s. Lee Iacocca, then president of the automobile giant Ford, had confirmed rumors that General Motors was planning to launch a new economy car it had been working on for more than a year. He demanded that Ford engineers beat their rival to the street with such a vehicle, giving them little more than a year to accomplish the task. It is commonly accepted that new car products take upwards of three years for research and development before being ready for consumers. Still, his mignons rose to the challenge and the compact Pinto was available for the public in the time he allotted.

Unfortunately, the vehicle had a basic defect. A bracket that secured the exhaust pipe was placed just under the gas tank. The top of this metal piece was shaped to a point. Under certain, low impact, rear end collisions, the bracket would be driven upward piercing the gas tank. The clash of metal on metal produced sparks that caused the small car to burst into flames, trapping occupants inside. Men, women and children would become engulfed in flames, dying agonizing deaths.

As time passed, lawsuits were started throughout the country on behalf of victims. For years, Ford officials were bombarded with demands for testing information. In response, they stated that the safety tests conducted before releasing the vehicle for sale to the public, had not turned up any indication of the defect. When forced by court order, Ford produced documents that they swore under oath, constituted all the tests that had been conducted. This pattern continued until an attorney in Lubbock, Texas, received a set of test results that varied from all those produced to other lawyers over the years. These documents, obviously provided to him in error, showed that a number of company tests had revealed the hazard. Explosions had occurred on Ford test sites and the company knew why.

Not only had Ford been aware of the danger, but subsequent documents revealed that management employees had analyzed the likelihood of lawsuits, estimated the number the company could expect and decided it would be cheaper to deal with the lawyers than to incur the cost and delay of stopping production and sale of the vehicles. The company had intentionally placed death traps on the road.

Concealment and destruction of self incriminating internal documents has been a traditional device by corporate giants in their attempts to avoid legal responsibility for their misdeeds. The advent of e-mail and hard drives has made those efforts more difficult but they still try.

Trial lawyers are aware of numerous similar situations involving some of America's premier corporations. Asbestos manufacturers spent four decades concealing the fact that their product was killing thousands of Americans each year. When confronted with lawsuits over the product, the companies settled them subject to confidentiality agreements that strictly prohibited the litigants, lawyers and their experts from revealing the dangers associated with their product. In one instance, the defendant corporation purchased the laboratory that had conducted studies for a plaintiff and buried all its research.

Tobacco companies denied cigarettes caused cancer, despite

their own research that showed the deadly and addictive forces of nicotine and, in at least one instance, intentionally increased the amount of that chemical to further insure smoker addiction. One company actually prepared a report for a European nation extolling the virtues of cigarette smoking, boasting it caused cancer and death, which could be counted upon to reduce that nation's burgeoning senior citizen population.

Medical devices that break after being implanted in humans remain on the market. Medicines that kill patients are marketed openly and corporate profits are freely spent on lawyers to defend the companies and politicians who are willing to push laws designed to protect them from their own misdeeds.

By definition, the judicial system is an adversarial process. Opposing sides advocate their positions before judge or jury. Adversaries line up to enter the arena and air their disputes. Somebody wins. Somebody loses. The judiciary is the civilized alternative to gunfights. Lawyers are the gunfighters of yore, only lawyers take money instead of human life. Without lawyers, the system would fail. Lawyers are human. Humans are greedy. The system caters to greed, and depends upon it for survival.

It is little wonder that business interests constantly seek to limit lawyer contingent fees. Lawyers with contingent fee agreements usually are called upon to advance the costs of litigation and are unable to collect any fee for their efforts if the cases do not result in favorable settlements or verdicts. In most cases, the lawyers cannot even recover their advanced costs unless they achieve a favorable verdict or settlement.

By limiting the amount of contingency fees, reducing the percentage of each award a lawyer can collect, corporate America can discourage attorneys from accepting such cases.

The love/hate relationship Americans have with lawyers manifests itself in newspapers, movies, television programs and literature. Lawyers are the American judicial system. Many have succeeded in politics, becoming legislators, governors and presidents. They are the judges. Congress and most state legislatures count more lawyers among their ranks than any other profession or career. More American presidents have possessed law degrees than any other advanced degree. Lawyers, judges and the judicial system they operate have an abundance of critics and admirers, many of whom come from the ranks of lawyers.

One proverb holds that, "A good lawyer must be a great liar." Shakespeare wrote, "The first thing we do, let's kill all the lawyers." The author Charles Lamb wrote, "He is no lawyer who cannot take two sides." Lawyer jokes rival blond jokes. While a majority of American lawyers do not actually participate in courtroom battles, those that do are the source of nearly all the attention, scorn or adulation.

Courtrooms become the battlegrounds where individuals advance their dreams of sudden wealth, and corporations and insurance companies jealously protect their bank accounts.

Since its inception, the American judicial system has been assailed by critics from all walks of life. Its defenders concede that it is flawed, but
hasten to point out that nobody has devised anything better. The core

of this dispute lies in the U.S. Constitution that states, "All men are created equal." At least they are supposed to have equal rights. The third branch of government was established to ensure and enforce this concept. Our founding fathers surely never contemplated citizens sitting as jurors in towering skyscrapers dealing with tragic automobile accident cases. Of course, they never contemplated skyscrapers and automobiles either.

Willie E. Gary, senior partner at Gary, Williams, Finney, et al. states, "This is America. In America, you have got to do the right thing." Gary stresses this at press conferences, in churches and before juries. "Some folks just plain don't read the Constitution. When that happens, somebody has to read it to them."

With one short statement, Willie Gary, again and again, summarizes the fundamental concept that has promised hope to millions, yet has been the bane to the rich and powerful. Gary has literally seen billions of dollars change hands. Americans have tried to abandon the lesson of their ancestors that, "might makes right." However, at the same time they have strictly adhered to another lesson from the past – "To the victor go the spoils." The rich no longer have a monopoly on greed; it can be exercised by everyone in America.

There is an old law school adage: the "A" students become trial lawyers, the "B" students become in-house company lawyers, and the "C" students become judges. They also learn details of how corporate America has teamed with lawyers on their dole to infect the judiciary with substandard jurists bent only on limiting the authority of courts and the ability of people to access them.

When I abandoned Michigan for the Florida sunshine, I was complaining bitterly about the method by which Michigan Supreme Court Justices were selected, and I continue to criticize that system, as well as the ongoing role played by political influence in all judicial selection practices.

In Michigan, the current selection process is one in which Michigan judges appear on the ballot as non-partisans, i.e. persons not affiliated with any political party or special interest group; however, the two major political parties nominate judges for a position on the ballot.

Republicans and Democrats pick the candidates and then they are dangled out to the voters as being non-partisan. Michigan is not alone in allowing politics to govern the selection of judges. Florida's record is not much better.

The method of selecting judges varies from state to state. Although some states have met with limited success in reducing the role played by political and special interests, this method continues to dominate the manner by which judges are selected to serve throughout the country. Of course, these activities do not usually occur in full public view; they often take place in secret.

A wealthy businessperson makes a substantial contribution to one political party or a particular candidate for high office, quietly suggesting that he would be pleased if his daughter would receive the next judicial office that becomes available. Special interest groups carefully screen candidates for whom they support financially, and they make their preferences known to those elected into office. These politicians will likely need help again in the future. The Chamber of

Commerce and the Trial Lawyers Association are prominent among groups that actively press elected officials when a judicial selection is pending. These two organizations represent opposite poles of political thinking and each clearly recognizes the value of a judge who is "friendly" to the value they represent.

Organizations that may have just a single issue to advocate often are amongst the most vocal, and they can provide significant financial help to candidates for any office. Mothers Against Drunk Driving (MADD) most recently has emerged as an influential voice in judicial selection, as have the anti-abortion organizations. Their singularity of purpose, however, risks the promotion of individuals who may be dedicated to their causes, but wholly incompetent to deal with the many other issues confronting judges every day. A judge who is relentless in sentencing every drunk driver to lengthy jail terms may not have the slightest idea how to deal with boundary disputes, child custody issues or malpractice questions.

Over the years, our presidents and state governors have consistently attempted to use their authority to try controlling the selection of judges or to select judges who will bend to their will.

The impact of this movement, both direct and indirect, is weighing heavily on a sharply divided Congress. President George W. Bush abandoned the traditional practice of seeking input from the American Bar Association about nominees to the Federal Courts. William H. Pryor, Jr., Alabama attorney general, who the President selected for the 11th Circuit Court of Appeals, best typifies this selection process.

As attorney general in Alabama, Pryor actively pursued

the execution of a mentally retarded man convicted of murder. He compared homosexual relations to sex with animals; and called Roe vs. Wade, the Supreme Court case permitting abortion, "the worst abomination of constitutional law in our history." Pryor also defended posting Bible quotes on a courthouse door and advocated repealing part of the Voting Rights Act, a law designed to insure equal access to the voting booth.

At age forty-one, Pryor has established himself as a close ally of big business. He refused to join other attorneys general across the nation in lawsuits against the tobacco industry stating, "The business community must be engaged heavily in the election process as it affects legal and judicial offices." He also founded the Republican Attorneys General Association, an organization that skirts campaign-financing laws by permitting large, anonymous donations from corporate giants used to finance his campaigns and those of other conservative attorneys general throughout the country. His organization and others like it have received over a million dollars from major companies including Wal-Mart, Home Depot and the insurance giant, AIG.

In George W. Bush's home state of Texas, a budding, young direct mail consultant emerged in the late 1980s to organize business leaders into a cohesive financing machine that successfully overthrew all the Democrats sitting on the Texas Supreme Court. Karl Rove had assumed the informal title of "Bush's brain." He was so successful in Texas that by its 1997-98 term the Texas Supreme Court had overturned 69 percent of jury verdicts favorable to plaintiffs and insurance companies. Doctors and pharmaceutical companies won nearly every case presented.

Rove's success was contagious. Nationally, the U.S. Chamber of Commerce joined with the Business Roundtable to establish a number of covert front groups that filtered corporate money into divisive judicial campaigns in Michigan, Idaho, Pennsylvania and Alabama. By the year 2000, the Chamber was able to claim victory in twenty-one of twenty-four judicial elections after funneling an estimated $45.6 million into judicial campaigns.

In most areas, judges remain in office from the time of their selection until retirement or death. Once entrenched, little can be done to effectively control or remove them. Most observers agree that competent judges are reluctant to speak out against incompetent judges for fear of creating some change that might jeopardize their own security in office. Well-qualified judges are equally protective of their own authority and will staunchly defend the right of a bumbling jurist to foist injustice after injustice upon the public. If a method is created to curtail atrocities by one impotent judge, that method could later be applied to them.

Such problems magnify when judges are called upon to decide cases without juror involvement. Divorce and custody issues usually do not involve juries; yet the number of domestic problems filed in our courts constitutes approximately one-half of all the cases filed in the United States. In such cases, the judges are granted wide discretion in their decisions, thus allowing them vast latitude in deciding the fate of children, rights of parents and even terminating a parent's rights to be a parent in many jurisdictions.

Some of the judges making such decisions have never had

children of their own. Others quietly confide that they despise the work, and rely entirely upon the bureaucrats and social workers assigned to them for the decision making in such matters. These often can be people that the parents never meet, some of whom are fresh out of college with nothing more than a degree and a new wardrobe to recommend them.

We will never take the political process completely out of the selection of judges. That simply cannot be achieved. Special interests have too much money and too much power to let that happen. We have to accept the fact that mediocre judges will last as long as our judicial system lasts, with judges who owe their jobs to somebody else. These men and women used special interest money to get elected or special interest power to get appointed, and they are expected to repay the favor over and over and over. Many of them will, and many of the remainder will apply their own personal views on an issue in dispute, not withstanding what the existing law had long established.

These often are the same special interest groups that want to limit the power of juries, if not eliminate juries altogether. They will tell the people that legal issues are just too complicated for the common man to understand, and that judges and super panels of experts are much better qualified for the task. What they are really saying is that average people are just not smart enough to decide these issues. Juries are made up of average people who don't know right from wrong; therefore, we need to eliminate them from the process.

These follow in the vein of the same special interest groups who just seventy-five years ago, said that women were not smart enough to vote, and less than a hundred years ago, said that it was all right for blacks to be segregated from whites in schools, neighborhoods, restaurants and even on buses. They are afraid of juries because they can't buy juries.

Having won the revolution against British tyranny, the Founding Fathers sought to install a government that would protect its citizens from the arbitrary whims of monarchs and their mignons. They ordained that elected legislators would adopt laws, elected administrators would enforce these laws, and an appointed judiciary would interpret the laws whenever their application was questioned. These concepts prevail in today's federal government; however, one universal concept remained in place and continues to remain in all fifty states, as well as in the federal system - the right to trial by jury.

The Founders reasoned that the best safeguard against tyranny was the right of all men to assert their grievances before members of their own society – their peers. These would be people from all walks of life: farmers, merchants, professionals and laborers. Such a procedure reasoned that the framers of our Constitution would ensure that government and the laws it adopted, would be subject to review by common people who were every bit as subjected to those laws, as the person seeking review. What was best for one would be best for all and how better to make that determination than select folks from the entire community to consider such questions.

This idea probably is every bit as good today as it was when Washington crossed the Delaware River. Ordinary people have to deal with the complications of modern life. Who better to decide how modern laws should apply to these complications and the individual problems they generate? And when those laws are violated, who better to determine the appropriate penalty for such violations? Thus, has arisen the basis for juries to decide what damages are appropriate when someone is physically, financially or emotionally injured by another who has disregarded the law.

It is no exaggeration that there are millions of pages printed in legal journals, newsletters, books and other tomes, that are devoted to assisting lawyers in jury selection for the cases they try. Many psychologists, social workers and other behaviorists devote their careers to assisting trial lawyers in jury selection. Others help operate mock trials designed to aid in predicting what points will be most helpful, or which most damaging when the real event takes place. In each trial, the issues, complex or simple, ultimately come down to a single question – "What do the jurors think?" Lawyers must determine what they can do to obtain the best possible jurors in each of his cases. Is it a science? Is it an art? Is it pure luck?

Most experts opine that African Americans, Hispanics and other minorities are more likely to have been victimized by police, factory layoffs, racial slur and other unpleasant events. As a result, the experts believe they possess a greater propensity to doubt police testimony, and be sympathetic to plaintiffs who have been injured, lost their jobs or have lost a loved one. Experts also believe minorities are more inclined to give large awards to the little guy; someone who faces the same daily miseries and injustices they perceive have been thrust upon them by an unkind society. Minorities are more likely to identify with an unemployed, African American factory worker, than a large corporation or a physician who probably lives in a big house in the suburbs. They are also far more likely to believe the exhortations of a minority lawyer then those of a white, Anglo-Saxon Protestant.

Jury tampering is a serious, criminal offense. No one is allowed to speak with jurors about a case while they are in trial. All juries in the country are warned not to discuss the case outside the jury room, at home with family or friends and are not to read anything about the case in newspapers or watch anything about it on television until after the case is over. Nobody knows how many jurors pay much attention to these instructions, but woe unto any lawyer or litigant who approaches a juror while the case is going on.

However, there are no such restrictions regarding attempts to influence members of society in general. Untold millions of dollars are spent every year by business and industry on media blitzes designed to convince Americans, almost all of whom are potential jurors that their jury system is running amok, destroying the American way of life. Bar associations and lawyers across the country spend comparable amounts trying to counter these efforts. The propaganda machines are churning endlessly. Disc jockeys are fed information about unusually high jury verdicts. Perhaps the most notorious such case was the McDonald's spilled coffee case, where a middle-aged woman received a verdict of millions when her carry-out coffee cup overturned dumping scalding liquid on her crotch.

Lawyers today usually are permitted to ask potential jurors if they have formed any preconceived views of the jury system. There are increasing reports of individuals who reply that they believe the system is out of control.

Sometimes a prospective juror will refer to the McDonald's case as an example. Most people do not know that the woman required several surgical procedures to treat her third degree burns over six percent of her body, including her inner thighs, perineum, buttocks and genital and groin areas. She was hospitalized for eight days, during which time she underwent skin grafting. She sought to settle her claim for $20,000 but McDonalds refused.

In that case the plaintiff was a passenger in her grandson's car and ordered coffee that was served in a Styrofoam cup at the drive through window of a local McDonalds. After receiving the order, the grandson pulled his car forward so his grandmother could add cream and sugar to her coffee. She placed the cup between her knees and attempted to remove the plastic lid from the cup. As she removed the lid, the entire contents of the cup spilled into her lap.

McDonalds said it held its coffee at between 180 and 190 degrees fahrenheit to maintain optimum taste. Other establishments sell coffee at substantially lower temperatures, and coffee served at home is generally 135 to 140 degrees. Documents produced by McDonalds showed more than 700 claims against the company for selling coffee that was heated well beyond industry and safety standards.

The jury awarded her $200,000 in compensatory damage. The jury also awarded her $2.7 million in punitive damages which equals about two days of McDonalds coffee sales. The award was subsequently reduced to $480,000 even though the judge called McDonalds' conduct reckless, callous and willful.

Critics of civil justice, who have pounced on this case, often charge that she was driving the car or that the vehicle was in motion when she spilled the coffee; neither is true. (source: Lectlaw.com)

Much of the misinformation relating to jury verdicts today is distributed through the internet. The proliferation of "true story" e-mails has disseminated more misinformation to the public that one could hardly conceive possible 200 years ago. This phenomenon is frequently observed in the process of jury selection in the attempt to find a juror with an open mind, almost a non-sequitur to day. One jury selection consultant recently suggested that the computer button "forward" should be outlawed or our society will shortly be reduced to a nation of dimwits, a result some claim already exists.

What has caused the proliferation of litigation unknown fifty years ago? Much of it can be blamed or credited to the inauguration of John F. Kennedy after World War II. When Kennedy became President he promised a new vision and a new horizon and he was determined to make legal services readily available to the poor, who by tradition have been barred from the courthouse door, because they were unable to hire lawyers. Prior to that era, lawyer advertising was severely restricted by rules of ethics promulgated by the established legal structure of old-line law firms. Advertising of any kind was prohibited for lawyers and, other than having your name listed in phone directories, no promotion was allowed. Your name could not appear in print larger than the standard type and as a young lawyer I strongly supported the change for some promotion for new lawyers believing that established law firms had a virtual monopoly that they wanted to continue.

Little did I realize that the relaxing of those rules would lead to what we see today. Lawyers now hawk their wares in ways I consider demeaning to the profession. Of course I am not sure it is a profession anymore, at least not in the traditional sense. The term profession was defined in the case of Commonwealth vs. Brown (20 NE 2nd 478, 4881 Mass. 1939) as a "learned profession characterized by the need of unusual learning, the existence of confidential relations, the adherence to a standard of ethics higher than that of the marketplace,…." . In our local phone directory, there are sixty pages in the yellow pages for lawyers with full-page ads, back and front covers and occupying one-tenth of the entire section.

Billboards adorn the highways offering free consultations and house calls. Recent television commercials are now running consecutively, three at a time during broadcast breaks and are reaching even lower extremes of professional insult. All of these ads are accompanied by disclaiming language in hardly observable print required by the duplicitous bar associations stating: "The hiring of a lawyer is an important decision that should not be based solely upon advertising."

The affect of such advertising upon prospective jurors, an incidental but most important intended aspect is largely ignored or glossed over by the "profession."

What you have just read will hopefully provide a foundation for the case narratives that are to follow and played out everyday in the courtrooms and boardrooms of America.

II

SEPARATE BUT UNEQUAL

I have learned that success is to be measured not so much by
the position that one has reached in life as by the obstacles
which he has overcome while trying to succeed.
BOOKER T. WASHINGTON 1859-1915

Willie E. Gary was born on a small farm just outside of Eastman, Georgia, on July 12, 1947. About the time of Willie's birth, Dr. Samuel Green was reincarnating the post war Ku Klux Klan just 140 miles north, in Atlanta, where his Association of Georgia Klan would take roots. It would temporarily spread throughout the Deep South, becoming particularly embedded in Florida.

Gary's life began harshly, nearly ending within days. He was one of twins born to Turner and Mary Gary, and the only one to survive. Both he and his mother required extensive hospitalization, incurring medical bills that forced his father to sell the family's small farm in south-central Georgia to pay the costs. He was the sixth child. In all, his parents would have eleven children, adding five more in the years that followed.

As soon as mother and child could endure the trip, Turner moved his family to a three-room shack in Canal Point, Florida, where Gary would spend most of his formative years. During those very years, Klan chapters were sprouting up throughout the area miming Dr. Green's Atlanta, white supremacist organization. The Gary family would scratch out a living harvesting sugar cane under the blistering sun. Their home was protected from the elements by a tarpaper roof. It had no electricity. There was no plumbing.

Each June, following the cane harvest, Gary's father would nail shut the windows and doors to their home and the family would embark upon the migrant trails. They traveled to camps in the Carolinas, where they would pick string beans, celery, sweet corn, cabbage and apples, returning to Florida in time to begin harvesting the winter crops from November through the winter and spring. By his tenth birthday, Gary was accomplished at picking each of the crops.

No one can doubt that his formative years were punctuated with severe deprivation, and he was raised in an atmosphere of extreme racial prejudice and discrimination. Opportunity was still only for white people. blacks only were suited for work in the fields, sweeping streets and cleaning toilets. They attended segregated schools, used different lavatories and rode in the back of the bus.

I was born during the depression years on the north side of Chicago. My father had a good job, considering the times, as a sales person for a wholesale grocery company headquartered in Chicago. We ate well. His territory included the entire state of Wisconsin, and when I was old enough my dad would frequently take me with him, driving throughout the state in a 1935 Nash automobile manufactured in

Kenosha, where we later moved. I enjoyed those trips and spent as much time with my father as I could. He was born in the upper peninsula of Michigan and enjoyed the outdoors, taking me with him on his many fishing trips, which I begged him to do.

My mother was not pleased that the hospital where I was born was then located in the heart of Chicago gangster land and the notorious Valentine's Day massacre took place just a few blocks away from my birthplace.

My grandparents had emigrated from Italy in the year 1900 and settled in a predominately Italian neighborhood in Chicago. Mother decided that I was to be raised "the American way," and we moved to Wisconsin at an early age where I was raised in a non-ethnic environment. Although my parents spoke Italian, they never spoke the language at home except during a discussion that I was not meant to understand. It didn't bother me at the time but in retrospect, I wish I had learned the language as it would have put me in good stead when I traveled to Italy years later with my family in search of distant relatives.

I became aware at an early age that Italians, then living in "wasp" neighborhoods, were objects of insults, derision and obscene name calling, so I was not totally immune from sympathy for the hateful attacks upon blacks that I observed in my later years.

I spent my early years of education in the public schools. Throughout her life, my mother was determined that I become well educated and by the third grade, they decided a parochial school environment was what I needed. My parents then joined the local Catholic Church, a surprising fact that they were not already members considering their Tuscan heritage.

I learned later that my grandfather was a violent anti-papist, which was not an unusual social position for him to take during Mussolini's era. None of my aunts or uncles on my mother's side had been raised in the Catholic religion. It is somewhat ironic that although raised and educated in the Catholic faith, I am not a practicing Catholic. I have developed a cynicism, resulting from my experiences during the war and exacerbated by subsequent and recent socio-political positions supported by religious extremists.

World War II was entering its third year when I started my senior year of high school. I was afforded the opportunity to enlist in a newly created special military program that provided a college education resulting in an officer commission. It was, as my parents confirmed, an offer too good to refuse; therefore, in lieu of being drafted I decided to apply for entrance to the program and after taking the required entrance exams, was accepted.

Within days after graduation from high school, I found myself on a train headed for the city of Detroit and entered classes at the University of Detroit. It was there, that I met Laurie, my wartime sweetheart, who later became my wife of over sixty years now. Those events, including my subsequent service in the battles of Europe, are related in the recently published *A Story of Love and War*.

I returned to Detroit after my discharge in 1946, married Laurie and re-enrolled at the University of Detroit, taking advantage of educational supplements granted to war veterans. I finished my undergraduate engineering studies that had been interrupted by the sudden termination of the program for which I had enlisted. Bored with engineering, I opted to continue my education by attending the Detroit College of Law, one of a handful of private schools started throughout the country during the depression years. The college was later merged with Michigan State University, and a sports stadium now occupies the former site of the college in downtown Detroit.

My first son, Robert Jr., was born in Grosse Pointe, Michigan, a month after Willie Gary's birth, as far removed by culture and distance from Eastman, Georgia, as one could imagine. I supported my fledging family by working on the assembly line at the General Motors truck and coach plant in the City of Pontiac, county seat of Oakland County.

At that time, Oakland County was home to the emerging elite of the automobile industry, and a conservative haven for white executives who fled Detroit after World War II when confronted by a growing, African American community. The black workers had been imported from Southern states during World War II to work in the city's industrial war plants. Following the war, these transplants chose to remain in Detroit, where wages and housing conditions far surpassed that which they had left behind in the Deep South.

While attending law school, I seized an opportunity to become a law clerk for Arthur E. Moore, a prominent, county probate judge. Upon passing the Bar Examination, I formed a partnership with Tom T. Reese whom I met in law school and we opened an office in downtown Pontiac in 1951, receiving enough assignments and referrals from my former employer to pay basic bills while establishing a law practice. Willie Gary had just passed his fourth birthday.

I had moved my growing family to Oxford, in northern Oakland County, where I would open another office. My brief years as a law clerk had afforded me the opportunity to befriend many attorneys who also were willing to send an occasional case my way.

Meanwhile, Gary was getting his first exposure to education, though working in the fields severely limited that opportunity. Like most children of migrant workers in Florida and the Carolinas where his family labored over the seasonal crops, he spent mornings in the fields and was picked up by bus for afternoons in segregated schools established for the transient children.

The popular concept of that era - that education was "separate, but equal," was a myth. Poorly trained African American teachers and a woeful lack of educational tools made providing an education beyond the most elementary level an impossible chore. Study by night was limited to the waning hours before sunset, since Gary lived without electricity, and work in the fields began at sunrise.

Gary's pursuit of education must have been the product of sheer will, as he had no real role models to mimic. Gary's stubborn drive for education was a precursor of things to come.

Gary returned to Florida from the Carolina apple fields ahead of his family in 1961, arriving home in September. That was the year he started high school. He already understood that there would never be enough money for him to attend college.

During those same years, I was busy building my law practice in Michigan. Laurie and I had four children and we had opted to live in the more rural, northern Oakland County area, where land was plentiful and large tracts could be purchased for reasonable sums. Most of the land was still being farmed. The small towns of that region were beginning to see significant population growth, necessitating changes in local government and the establishment of new business to serve the growing number of residents. This would afford me the opportunity to grow my law practice with the community. I continued to be active in local organizations and enjoyed a good reputation with my fellow lawyers and local judges. In 1965, I was sworn in as president of the Oakland County Bar Association. Later I would serve on the Michigan State Bar Association's Board of Commissioners, elected by my fellow attorneys in Oakland County to represent their interests on the statewide governing body.

Young Willie Gary was readying himself for college during the summer months of 1967 and applied for a football scholarship at Bethune-Cookman College. I continued focusing on my law practice in the suburbs of Detroit. I was isolated from the racial unrest simmering in the Motor City just about forty miles south of my office.

On July 12, 1965, officers from the Detroit Police Department Vice Squad raided an after hours bar on 12th Street, where more than eighty people were celebrating the return of two black Viet Nam veterans. Such a raid sparked a neighborhood disturbance. The disturbance escalated to isolated looting and fire bombing. The violence spread through much of the city, leaving 43 people dead, 1,189 injured and over 7,000 people arrested. African American Detroit residents, by that time more than 40 percent of the city's population, had suffered years of police brutality, such as four-man police squads intimidating teenagers on the streets calling them "boy" and "nigger," as well as administering random beatings to innocent pedestrians.

Laurie and I, with our children, were in the city on a family boating holiday weekend on the Detroit River before the violence commenced and it began to spread while we were there. We were forced to travel through the troubled areas on our return to our home and we saw armored vehicles and National Guard soldiers on patrol with automatic weapons slung over their shoulders.

Crowds were gathering at busy street intersections. I was very uncomfortable and felt threatened for the safety of my family. In so many ways, it was a reminder of my war experiences with the Ninth Army as we left bombed out cities of Europe in our wake with smoke billowing from the ruins. I felt lucky again, as I had years earlier, as we escaped to the safety of the secure suburbs.

These riots followed the Watts riots in Los Angeles, California, by just under two years. In the years that followed, I would find myself seated next to famed criminal defense attorney, Johnny Cochran, in an Orlando, Florida courtroom pitted against entertainment giant, the Disney Company. An interesting parallel existed long before that day between us, one born of racial unrest and rioting.

Cochran told of four thousand African Americans in Los Angeles needing lawyers to defend them on a myriad of charges stemming from the riots. Cochran was not the first prominent trial lawyer to come to defend blacks in racially charged cases. In 1926, famed lawyer Clarence Darrow was called upon to defend a black on a murder charge arising out of a racially charged event arising in the city of Detroit. Darrow, probably the most celebrated lawyer of the 20th century, was notable as a defender of the underdog and civil rights.

The two most famous trials in which he participated took place in the 1920s. The first of these trials was the notorious Leopold-Loeb tried in Chicago in 1924. He saved Nathan Leopold and Richard Loeb from execution but not prison, for the murder of fourteen-year-old, Bobby Franks.

A year later, Darrow defended high school teacher, John T. Scopes, in the famous, "monkey trial." Scopes was charged with violating Tennessee law by teaching evolution. In 1926, Darrow found himself defending Ossian Sweet, a black Detroit doctor charged with the murder of a white member of a mob attempting to remove Sweet and his family from their home. The circumstances leading to the case are remarkably similar to the events leading to the Detroit riots thirty years later. The following are the words written by Darrow about the case:

The facts were simple. Up to the beginning of the war, Detroit had some twelve thousand Negroes. There, as everywhere, they were packed into the lowliest and the dirtiest quarters. When the war in Europe broke out, the people of America saw their opportunity to serve humanity and get rich. Detroit enjoyed an unprecedented demand for automobiles. So, the manufacturers sent south for Negro labor. Most of these men and their families remained in Detroit after the World War was over and we were freed from Germany.

The Negro workmen could stay in the automobile factories in the daytime, but they had no place to stay at night, so they expanded the Negro section, and some of them moved out to what was called the white districts. Many of the Negroes in Detroit were old-time citizens. By degrees, the Negroes became citizens of Detroit, and amongst them are doctors, lawyers, and many others of marked mentality. In the early days, Detroit and other Northern cities were friendly to Negroes; but that was a long time ago.

The negroes were not the only people who came from the South to the North during the war. White workmen as well as colored ones, came up to all our industrial centers. The whites brought with them their deep racial prejudices, and they also brought with them the Ku Klux Klan. In Detroit the Klan was strong.

I had determined not to get into any more cases that required hard work and brought me into conflict with the crowd. I had fought for the minority long enough. I wanted to rest, but to rest would be something new. But I could not rest. I get tired of resting. And something always comes along to disturb my restful contemplations, anyhow, so - I was in New York, and a committee of Negroes came to see me. I knew they were Negroes because they told me so. In color and intelligence, they were like many of the most intelligent white men that I know.

This committee wanted to engage my services to defend

eleven Negroes in Detroit, on the charge of murder. Doctor Ossian Sweet, the main defendant in the case I was undertaking, was a man of strong character. He began his career in Detroit as a bell hop on the lake boats plying between that city and Cleveland, after which he took all sorts of odd jobs such as fall to the man whose face is black. By a hard struggle he worked his way through college, and then through the medical school at Ann Arbor. When he had completed his years of study, he opened an office in Detroit. In the meantime he had married, and had a child about two years old at the time that he was arrested for murder.

Doctor Sweet had been living in congested quarters with his wife's family, and for some time had been looking for a place that he could buy. But as soon as the neighborhood found out that Doctor Sweet, the owner, was a colored man, they proceeded to band together into what they called an "Improvement Association," of which practically every one in that locality became a member, and a meeting was held in a schoolhouse, at which the speakers made dire threats as to what would happen if a negro should settle in their street.

Again night came on; again the throng gathered around the house, increasing in number and restlessness. The colored men were standing watch at the various windows windows with guns in hand, as the mob came swarming toward the place. A volley of stones was thrown toward the house, and two of the windows were broken. Thereupon shots were fired from inside the windows, and the crowd moved back; at once the policemen entered the house, and took all the inmates to the police station. It soon transpired that one man had been killed and another wounded by the fusillade.

As might be expected, the feeling in Detroit was strong against the accused. Few colored men in America charged with killing white persons have ever lived to tell the tale; they have been lucky if they survived long enough to be tried in court under the forms of law and legally slaughtered.

It was not easy to get a jury. I kept wondering what a white man would think of his chances for getting a fair trial in Africa if he had killed a Negro and was placed on trial before twelve men with black faces. After considerable time we managed to get twelve men who said they could be fair, but of course, they knew nothing about that. No one knows so little about a man's ability to be fair as the man himself. To a man himself all his opinions, attitudes and prejudices are fair or he would not hold them. But no one ever wanted a fair juror; at least, no lawyer ever did.

After two trials that riveted the attention of Detroit, and indeed the nation, Darrow won the case before an all white jury and wrote of that victory years later stating:

My long sympathy for the colored people conspired to help me make one of the strongest and most satisfactory arguments that I ever delivered. The jury was not long in returning a verdict of acquittal. The verdict meant simply that the doctrine that a man's house is his castle applied to the black man as well as to the white man. If not the first time that a white jury had vindicated this principle, it was the first that ever came to my notice.

The defense of this case gave me about as much gratification as any that I have undertaken. While I was certain that my clients were right and that they were grievously wronged, I never had any sense of resentment against the community. The people who sought to drive that colored family from their home were only a part of the product of the bitterness bred through race prejudice, for which they were not responsible. So long as this feeling lives, tragedies will result. [1]

Judicial "tragedies" continue even until this day. Deliberate attempts to exclude blacks from juries by prosecutors and lawyers for insurance companies and corporations existed on the sole basis of race and continue, in some degree, even to this day. Although that practice is still attempted, it is now severely restricted and until recently, was a common and judicially endorsed occurrence.

Darrow, the first "Giant Killer" and champion of the underdog, continues to be an inspiration for trial lawyers who continue to believe, as did our founding fathers, that our jury system with all its imperfections is still the best protection in all of history for the rights of the common man.

I had joined the massive migration of whites to the northern suburbs of Detroit, where only a few blacks lived in close, segregated

[1] Clarence Darrow, *The Story of My Life*. Published by Buccaneer Books, Inc. © 1932

areas and were largely unnoticed by the majority of Oakland County residents who, just a decade earlier, had fled the growing African American community in Motor City. When World War II ended, black workers from the south had opted to remain in the city where they had labored manufacturing weapons for American armed forces. During the 1950s, the northern suburbs were among the nation's fastest growing communities.

General Motors had established a large truck manufacturing plant in Pontiac, the seat of Oakland County government. After WWII, the GM facility expanded its production capacity, attracting a number of African
American laborers to the city, with homes congregated primarily in the city's older, southern section.

They had little demand for legal services and few white lawyers were interested in handling those matters with which they did need assistance. A somewhat peaceful coexistence prevailed. Geography dictated separate schools. The African American residents attended their own churches, movie theaters and ate at restaurants within the borders of their own community.

There were just a handful of African American lawyers in the county, mostly in the city of Pontiac. It is my recollection that they represented the small, black community in that city, mostly laborers from the auto plants. There never seemed to be any trouble with race relations, at least any that I perceived.

That de facto harmony crashed in 1967 with the Detroit riots. Detroit is only forty miles south of Pontiac and several communities had grown up between the two cities. Expressways made it possible to travel downtown in a matter of fifty minutes or so.

By 1967 my firm was representing General Motors Acceptance Corporation. Initially our work involved subrogation cases resulting from automobile insurance damage claims, and repossessions of automobiles from delinquent customers. Many of the defendants were black. I became well acquainted with the local black attorneys and enjoyed an early rapport with them. This probably resulted from the fact that I was young and just starting out, as most of them were, and did not belong to a "silk stocking" prestigious law firm. That resulted in a familiarity and comfort with the blacks that I enjoy to this day. I was personally aware of the discrimination fostered upon my grandparents, immigrants from Italy in 1900. I'm sure those recollections added to my empathy for the African American struggle to achieve equality in our society; however, nothing in Michigan would ever compare to what I later was to witness in Florida.

Willie Gary failed to get the scholarship at Bethune-Cookman College and after three weeks of tryouts in August, 1967, the coach told him to go home. While he surely was disappointed, he was undaunted. He called upon his high school coach for help. The coach promised to call his friend who coached the football team at Shaw University in Raleigh, North Carolina. Relying on nothing more than that promise, Gary caught a bus to Raleigh.

Upon arrival at Shaw, he was told that the coach there had never heard of him. Furthermore, the field was full of players who had been invited to try out for the team and Gary had not even applied for admission to Shaw. Once again, he was told to go home. He refused. Instead, he mooched food from players at their residence hall, slept on the couch there and started showing up in the locker room every morning to clean the place. This went on for a few days until he was discovered by the coach and again, was told to go home.

In the meantime, Gary had applied for admission and managed to get a secretary at his high school to ship his transcripts to the admissions office. His paperwork was then in order. Upon learning this, the coach gave him a meal ticket good for just a few days and allowed him to show up on the practice field to watch the scrimmages until he could arrange transportation home. A player was hurt one day. The coach told him to fill in. Gary sacked the quarterback, blocked two punts and joined the team that afternoon. That entitled him to the scholarship necessary for his tuition, room and board.

After a year of classes at Shaw University, Gary returned to Indiantown where he married his high school sweetheart, Gloria Royal. He first met Gloria when she was five years old. Her father also was a migrant farmer. She also was one of eleven children. While he had been at Shaw, she had attended a local, junior college. They moved to an apartment near Raleigh where she enrolled at Shaw, going on to earn a degree in psychology.

As always, money was tight. Gloria tutored his teammates while Willie took jobs waiting on tables, washing dishes and working as a short order cook. One such job was a summer position at the Pelican Hotel in Stuart, Florida. Years later, after the hotel had fallen into disrepair, he would buy the building and convert it into his present, multi-million dollar offices.

The Detroit riots resulted in statewide efforts to improve race relations. These echoed a national trend that had been settling in for more than a decade, which meant reduced discrimination in housing and education. The landmark United States Supreme Court in Brown vs. Board of Education had struck down traditional acceptance of "separate but equal" education.

During the late 1960s, a federal judge ordered the Pontiac schools to start busing students across the city to achieve greater racial balance in the classrooms.

My practice flourished. We represented builders who were snapping up land for homes and shopping centers to serve new area residents. Expanding school districts that were enlarging their facilities and local municipalities were among our clients.

Most lawyers never forget the ordeal of their Bar Examinations. Florida has been notorious for having one of the most difficult such tests in the country. All prospective lawyers must pass their state's Bar Examination before being allowed to hang out a shingle. Prior to 1948, however, Florida had the unique and remarkably discriminatory practice relating to blacks. The law was then, if you were a white resident of Florida and attended and graduated from a Florida law school, you would be forthwith admitted to the Florida Bar. On the contrary, blacks were not allowed to attend law schools in the State of Florida and were required, if they desired to be a

Florida lawyer, to attend out of state law schools. In which case they, and only they, had to take The Florida Bar Examination.

The University of Florida outlines part of that base southern history in a recent publication entitled, "Milestones in University of Florida African American History," which states:

> In April 1949 Virgil D. Hawkins, a former faculty member of Bethune-Cookman College, applied for admission to the University of Florida College of Law school.
>
> In May of 1949, the University of Florida, through the Florida Board of Control (later Board of Regents), denied his admission (as well as five other African American graduate school applicants) based solely upon race.
>
> In 1954 the United States Supreme Court ordered the public schools desegregated "with all deliberate speed" by 1956 in Brown v. Board of Education and in a companion decision ordered the University of Florida to admit Virgil Hawkins. However, Virgil Hawkins was still not admitted to the University of Florida. After a successful appeal, at the age of 70 Mr. Hawkins took his oath of office and became a member of The Florida Bar by special waiver.
>
> Virgil D. Hawkins, Esq. can now rest proud. Along with other civil rights lawyers of his time, his efforts contributed to the breaching of barriers that allowed an African American lawyer to become our nation's 44th president.

I JUST WANTED TO RETIRE

It is not best to swap horses while crossing the river.
Abraham Lincoln

The discrimination against black lawyers that still existed in such recent times, was not known by me when I first joined Willie Gary, but it did not take long for me to realize that there was an animosity and discrimination that existed then and even today to some degree, although obviously lessened.

The Florida Bar Association, like bar associations in all fifty states, is a morass of antiquated regulations struggling to survive in modern American society. These associations cling to their desire for respect, despite an era of glaring television commercials, full-page advertisements in every local telephone directory, and direct mail brochures hawking lawyer services like pizzas and escort services. Yet most admission oaths administered to new attorneys demand a promise that they will pursue their chosen profession, "without regard to lucre."

These associations seem to believe lawyers were once perceived as professionals dedicated solely to the preservation of justice in America, with little or no regard for monetary gain. This perception bears little resemblance to the American layman's view of lawyers at any time in history, probably because it was just as false then as it is today; yet, leaders of these organizations seem to gain a great deal of comfort in the hypocrisy. In short, they yearn for "the good old days," with little or no acknowledgment that those bygone times were the epitome of exclusivity. The number of African American lawyers practicing law in "the good old days," in Florida, could be counted on one hand, if any could be found at all. As the southern author, William Faulkner, said of the time, "The past is not dead. In fact, it's not even past."

Gary graduated from North Carolina School of Law in 1974. When Gary took his examination, black students still typically failed the test as often as four or five times before finally gaining admission. Most white students passed it the first time. Gary studied eighteen hours a day. He passed on his first attempt.

While waiting for his test results, Gary tried finding a job as a law clerk or paralegal. There were no black law firms in the Stuart area. He seldom made it past the reception room at the white firms where he applied. He ended up working for the Stuart public defender's office, where he was paid twenty-five dollars a week for more than three months. When he learned he had passed the examination and was admitted to practice law in December 1974, he still was paid twenty-five dollars per week.

Back in Michigan, my practice was flourishing. I had been lawyering for more than twenty years and enjoying an excellent professional and community reputation. Approaching my fiftieth birthday, I knew every judge in the county by his first name and found myself comfortably settled in my community as a gentleman attorney and civic leader. My children were finishing high school and heading for college. I made an unsuccessful bid for state representative, attempting to unseat an older, experienced incumbent, perhaps signaling some discontent with my routine. Fortunately, for my future career, I lost the race. At this time, I was representing a company in Michigan that manufactured farm silos. It was the largest manufacturer of concrete silos in the Midwest. The company owned a large orange grove in Broward County, Florida, adjacent to Alligator Alley and decided to sell the property. I went to Ft. Lauderdale to conclude the sale.

The closing took place in Ft. Lauderdale at the buyer's lawyer's office in downtown Ft. Lauderdale. The office was on the tenth floor, overlooking the ocean and the New River, which winds through the city along Los Olas Boulevard, the center of social life in the city. The courthouse was within walking distance, as were luxury hotels, restaurants and boutiques. I marveled at the view and thought what a beautiful place this would be to practice law, compared to stodgy Michigan. The lawyers, other than me, were all dressed in casual attire, Gucci loafers, sans socks and Ralph Lauren, Polo shirts. They conversed easily among themselves about their boating, fishing and golfing adventures. As I was able to glance at all the closing statements, my eyes spun like the wheels of a slot machine when I saw what they were receiving from their clients for fees and the cost of title insurance policies, which lawyers in Florida were allowed to write, contrary to what was happening in Michigan. "This is the place to be for sure," I day-dreamed to myself, "a lawyer's paradise." That experience played a most important part in forming my decision to move to Florida.

How could I have comprehended that thirty-five years after that experience, I would be living for two months in the luxury hotel on the river, overlooking the ocean, in the same hotel that I observed during the real estate closing. Then later, trying a lawsuit in that same courthouse that I saw on that day, against one of the largest corporate giants in the world, Motorola Corporation.

I decided to take the Florida Bar Exam and passed it in 1978. I had no idea if I would ever use the Florida license, though it did come in handy a few times when a Michigan client would get involved in some transaction in Florida. I remember asking Florida lawyers what they thought of the idea of a man my age taking the Bar Exam. They all told me not to bother. It was too hard. There wasn't enough work to go around. There was no future for new lawyers in Florida. I learned later that Florida is a great place for lawyers. You can be as busy as you want to be. One thing I certainly never envisioned, is what would actually happen to me after I met Willie E. Gary.

I always led an active life. In addition to golf and sailing, I was an avid skier. On a particularly frigid Michigan day in January 1980, I dragged Laurie to a nearby ski resort for an afternoon outing. She kept me company as far as the lodge, but drew the line there. Her skis would stay on the car. Undaunted, I climbed on a chair lift to ascend the highest and most difficult run. Midway up the lift stalled.

The wind was cutting through my brand new ski parka like a cold scalpel through tissue paper. The chair drifted in the wind. My mind drifted to Florida. I could have been out fishing or playing golf. I was fifty-two years old. I was a successful lawyer, businessman and real estate developer. I had held high office in both my local and state bar associations. The lift finally got me to the top. I skied down the hill and went straight to Laurie in the lodge. I announced that now was the time for us to make the move. "That's fine, Bob," she said. "Would you like a hot drink? Your lips are blue."

The decision to move was made during the prior year, at which time I traveled to Florida several times to choose where we would spend our retirement years. I was familiar with Ft. Lauderdale and rejected it because of its congestion and busy life style. Someone had mentioned that Stuart, Florida, would be a fine place to reside with its excellent golf courses and waterways. It had easy access to the ocean through the St. Lucie Inlet and I had a desire to cruise to the Bahamas by pleasure boat, and fish and dive the beautiful reefs abundant there.

During a visit to Stuart, I visited the courthouse and sat in on a court proceeding. When I walked into the courtroom I was amazed to see, rather than the scales of justice behind the bench, as prevalent in Michigan courtrooms, a mounted sailfish of monstrous size, the now well-known trademark of Stuart. The traditional black robe did not adorn the judge's shoulders and the lawyers leaned on the bench casually discussing the amount the bank's lawyer should receive as his fee on a mortgage foreclosure of a residential home. Michigan was limited, by law, to a modest statutory fee of five hundred dollars, which was the maximum then. Here, they were talking in the thousands. This was indeed, I thought, a lawyer's paradise. I had little anticipation of what would really lie ahead.

I made a deposit on a condo the very next day after that courtroom experience and looked forward to catching my first sailfish. It did not take long, and it, albeit of modest size, now adorns my den wall.

I often discuss my decision to leave Michigan in terms of seeking a more leisurely life, one with fewer demands and greater opportunity to enjoy the comforts I could well afford. It is not my nature to be openly critical; however, it seems there was another, perhaps stronger reason for my departure. I was unhappy with the changes I witnessed all around me.

The mass migration of people from Detroit had imposed radical changes in my environment. I was forced to deal with issues imposed by the increased diversity of my community's residents. During my practice, I had drafted zoning laws for some of my neighboring communities; laws regulating the way people could use their land. Whenever anyone resisted these restrictions, I found myself in court forcing the unwanted limitation upon them. The judicial system had become far more formal and rigid. Gone were the days when the local justice of the peace court convened in the back of a barber shop where the constable cut hair while court was in session. The need for increased revenue caused ever-increasing tax burdens on my neighbors and me. Labor disputes were pouring into the streets.

I was chairman of the draft board during the Viet Nam and Korean conflicts and later I was called upon to defend a city in a claim by an honorably discharged Korean War veteran requesting reinstatement to his former job upon his release from the army, as required under existing law for veterans of a "war." The city insisted that I defend the case on the grounds that he was not entitled to reinstatement, because he was not a veteran of an officially declared "war," as required under the law; therefore, he was not entitled to a reinstatement. The judge ruled in our favor on that technicality. In looking back, I now believe that a jury of citizens would have ruled in the veteran's favor based upon common sense, a trait unknown to many judges.

During my last days in Michigan, Jim Sherman, the editor of our local newspaper, the "Oxford Leader/Orion Review," asked for an interview for a story to be published about my thirty-year career and why I suddenly was leaving it all behind. Jim was a long time personal friend of mine and was also the publisher and owner of the paper. He was a veteran of the war, fishing and hunting buddy, and we socialized frequently together. I agreed to the interview and the article was published in the newspaper on October 20, 1982, just days after I had moved to Stuart, Florida. It was entitled "RVP - Our Lawyer for 30 Years," with my picture included. It covered over two full pages of the newspaper and I was pleased that Jim provided me that honor. The story began reciting fond memories of my early years as a lawyer, when I was one of two attorneys in the entire community. Then, as I explained my decision to leave, I turned surprisingly bitter. My statements were as follows:

"First, I think Michigan has found itself controlled by single interest and pressure groups, the result of which, as

Will Rogers once put it, that 'everyone has a lobbyist but the average man.' We have engaged in political hypocrisy where we find that the highest justices of our state are nominated at political conventions but then run as non-partisans.

"We find public employees engaging in strikes, euphemistically called work stoppages, which are declared by state statute to be illegal. We see a government that taxes small businesses based upon their gross receipts whether they make a profit or not, a state government that juggles its books to show a paper balance as required by our Constitution and a state gambling system that generates millions when penny ante poker is outlawed. It is not difficult to understand under these circumstances why there is so little respect for the law. I think I can sum it up as one older and wiser lawyer than I, told me the other day at the court house when we discussed the changes in the practice of law in the past thirty years, when he said, "Bob, it just does not seem as much fun anymore.""

These comments, perhaps more than anything I may say today, likely explain why I fled Michigan and, thereafter, was attracted to Willie E. Gary and the opportunity to help "the average man" in struggles against government and big business. Regrettably, the cynicism I expressed back then has manifested itself again in even greater degree, and my permanent retirement after the last twenty years is not with any particular pride for being known as a "Giant Killer," as the following pages should disclose.

A PARTNERSHIP – OF SORTS

Good counselors lack no clients.
Shakespeare, Measure for Measure, Act 1, scene 2.

Gary opened his first office in Stuart in January 1975, after leaving the public defender's office. Like most new lawyers, he spent his first year handling small commercial disputes, defending in criminal cases and handling some divorce matters; however, during his second year, he was retained by a woman whose husband, a truck driver, had been decapitated in an automobile accident. The couple was African American. The case was filed in Putnam County, near the Georgia border. It was home to one of Florida's more active Ku Klux Klan chapters. Gary demanded $35,000 to settle the matter but was offered only $20,000. The case went to trial and the jury returned a verdict for exactly what he requested. The verdict brought him some attention and more negligence cases started coming his way, mostly African American clients who felt more comfortable with a lawyer of their own race.

By 1977 Gary, still a sole practitioner, had negotiated his first million dollar settlement and had decided to focus his efforts entirely on personal injury matters. He purchased a small office building on the St. Lucie River and began dreaming of building the largest all black law firm in America. In 1980, Lorenzo Williams, his friend and classmate at Shaw University, joined him.

We completed our family move from Michigan and I had opened an office across the street from the courthouse and was beginning to acquire a modest practice, just enough to continue my interest in the law while permitting adequate time to participate in the many pleasures Florida afforded, including boating, fishing and golf.

It was the Christmas season of 1980 and I was invited to a party hosted by Gary at his small, waterfront office. It was the prelude to the massive, modern Christmas parties at his present deluxe offices only doors down the street. These attract celebrities from throughout the country. There is an admission charged now, a gift for needy children. Back then it was a small, open house affair he hosted for local lawyers and for judges who might like a free drink before heading home.

Gary was dressed in nautical attire. He always has been a snappy dresser and I recall he was wearing a double-breasted, blue blazer with white trousers. He also was wearing some sort of captain's hat, jauntily tilted to one side. He was already beginning to gain a reputation as an aggressive trial lawyer; not necessarily a good thing at that time in Stuart, as his specialty was personal injury work. Stuart is a conservative community, with sympathies leaning more toward business than common folks.

We chatted at the party about my background and joked around quite a bit. In all, we hit it off very well. Little did I dream what lay in the future.

About a year passed, during which time I had contracted with a local building company to construct a new home. We were friendly with the owners of the company and Laurie and I played golf with them frequently at their local country club.

I began handling some minor legal matters for them and one day while on the golf course, they turned to me and asked if I knew a lawyer by the name of Willie Gary. They had been involved in a business venture with relatives that went sour and had hired an established, local firm to start a lawsuit, which they did and lost. The decision had been reversed by a higher court, however, and the second time around they had retained Gary. They felt he needed some assistance in the retrial of the case and asked me if I would look it over. I agreed, and upon reviewing the transcripts of the first trial, determined that the second trial would have a far more favorable result - if properly handled.

Upon learning this, they asked me to intercede in the case with Gary. I agreed subject to Gary's approval. It came readily.

Just a day or two later, Gary called me at my office. He was happy I was becoming involved and immediately asked me to take the case over. My first impression of Gary was that he was not particularly comfortable with commercial law or bench trials where the final decision rests with the judge, as was the case here. He was a trial lawyer whose focus was handling juries in personal injury matters. His forte is jury work, where he can talk with plain and simple people.

I took over the case, and worked through their Ft. Pierce office hand-in-hand with Lorenzo Williams. I handled the depositions, argued legal matters to the court, and drafted the pleadings, and when it came down to the trial, ended up with that as well. Gary was there, but he took little part in the proceedings.

We won the case after a three or four day trial. Walking from the courtroom, Gary threw his arm around my shoulder and said, "Man, you did a great job Bob, you saved us big time. I am going to buy your lunch."

About a week later, I received the invitation for lunch with Gary and Williams. We met at a small seafood restaurant in Stuart at the foot of the Roosevelt Bridge, which spans the St. Lucie River between Stuart and Jensen Beach to the north. It sported an informal, nautical atmosphere and was popular with local lawyers, judges and others associated with the local courts.

It was an affable meeting, telling jokes and war stories, revisiting our recent victory with all the usual relish. Much of the meal was laced with mirth and by the time the table was cleared we were in a well relaxed mood.

Out of the blue, Gary turned to me and said, "Bob - Lorenzo and I want you to become our partner." I was shocked, as the thought had never occurred to me. They were on a fast track and I certainly was not. I was not at all interested and told them so. They were much younger than I, and I knew I could never keep up with them.

We told a few more jokes and, for some reason I still cannot comprehend, I suggested that I might be willing to join them and be associated as "Of Counsel," a nebulous term used often by lawyers to denote a lawyer "emeritus," as one who was retired but still involved with the law in some degree. It was a term that appealed to me and seemed appropriate to my original intention in moving to Florida.

They insisted, however, that I should become an active partner and perhaps because I was envious of the view from their offices situated on the banks of the St. Lucie River, I began listening to their inducements. I began listing certain conditions, one of which was that my office would be overlooking the wide waters. They agreed and I continued with additional conditions, including one that Laurie would continue as my secretary, and they would pay her, something I had neglected to do. I would receive no salary or draw, but fees would be paid based on income produced and results obtained from trial successes. Every request made met with "no problem." We shook hands and I moved into the offices within a month. I had been practicing law in Florida for all of two years.

It did not take long for me to have second thoughts, though I never seriously thought to act upon them. I noticed many white lawyers were cool toward me, and men and women as well with whom I thought I had formed friendships.

One local lawyer said they made me a partner so they would have a respectable chauffeur. Several others called me Willie's token. Laurie and I received fewer invitations to social events. In addition to associating with black lawyers, I had come from Michigan and still considered an outsider.

In truth, I learned early on that Florida lawyers did not welcome Michigan lawyers for the simple reason that most local lawyers were woefully inadequate compared to their more out of state aggressive counterparts. This difference became increasingly apparent as I prepared Gary for trial after trial, noting our opposition usually was unprepared for the onslaught we laid at their doorsteps.

Shortly after making my move, Gary sought my help in an automobile accident case in Jacksonville, Florida. A truck ran a red light, seriously injuring a young sailor, when it plowed into the side of his car. A black legal affairs officer at a nearby naval base referred the case to Gary. Lorenzo and I handled all trial preparation, occasionally reporting the status to Gary, who took lengthy notes, a habit that persists to the present.

I was first to arrive at court on the trial date. The defense attorney, a partner from a large law firm, was next to arrive. He was a tall, thin, good-looking man in his middle forties. We chatted amiably until Willie and Lorenzo arrived. His attitude changed immediately. His disdain was apparent from that point forward, positioning himself as far from my black partners in the courtroom as possible, directing what few civil comments he made to me.

The sailor had been treated at the University of Michigan Hospital
in Ann Arbor by a famous orthopedist. I traveled to Michigan and took the doctor's deposition to be shown to the jury at the trial. The testimony was video taped, a technique just coming into use and a very effective trial tool. The x-rays of shattered bones and the hardware used by the surgeon in keeping them together were extremely graphic when shown on the screen in a darkened courtroom. The impact on the jurors and their resulting shock was apparent. The case proceeded well for us and the day for the closing argument to the jury arrived.

We had expended many hours the night before in preparing Gary for his closing argument but we could not agree on the dollar amount we should ask from the jurors. Until this time, Gary never had achieved a million dollar verdict; nor had many other lawyers at that time. Considering the severity of the sailor's injuries, I suggested the case was worth at least that amount and, finally, we agreed Gary would demand one million dollars.

Gary's closing argument was a classic of jury rhetoric. It was the first time I had witnessed his skills in a full jury trial. The jury listened to his every word, often displaying by their body language, apparent agreement. The defense made no objection, seemingly in a daze. I was to observe that characteristic often in later trials. When Gary is on a roll, defense lawyers have just not been able to stop him.

Gary stated, "Just remember members of the jury, this young man dreamed of serving his country and the defendant, Multi State Trucking Company, has denied that dream to him forever and that's just not right. He will never be able to be gainfully employed nor enjoy the pleasures of life to which by law, he is entitled. One million dollars members of the jury, not a penny less but you could give him more...."

The jury was out for less than two hours, before returning a verdict for $1,000,400. Gary put his head down on the counsel table and his tears of victory flowed.

On our way back home, a drive across the state, we stopped at every crossroads to continue celebrating. Laurie still remembers my demeanor during that memorable event, and reminds everyone present at social gatherings, how useless I was in the move to our new home that weekend. I did not do a single thing to help except walk around with my head in the clouds and a drink in my hand.

It was the beginning of two decades of one legal history making episode after another, as Gary and I marched forward to cases that yielded tens of millions of dollars and Willie E. Gary became recognized as probably the finest jury trial lawyer in the country.

Albeit there were times, expressed hereafter, as to the veracity of the traditional court system, of self-doubt, purpose and conflicts. Similar in some degree, to my war experiences of sixty years earlier. It was an experience that few lawyers could ever hope to encounter in a lifetime.

V

THE TRIAL
JEREMIAH J. O'KEEFE, SR. et al vs.
THE LOEWEN GROUP, INC., et al

Representative government and trial by jury are the heart and
lungs of liberty. Without them we have no other fortification
against
being ridden like horses, fleeced like sheep, worked like cattle,
and fed and clothed like swine and hounds.
JOHN ADAMS, 1774

Until early 2003, Mississippi was a haven for tort lawyers; the place where class actions against major corporations yielded huge settlements paid by drug companies and major manufacturers of numerous defective products. It was a place where large verdicts often were rendered against big business. Mississippi's laws and the jurors, usually from low-income families and often African American, proved time and again to be insurmountable for the slick, corporate attorneys. These attorneys were imported to defend claims of death and permanent disability caused by companies that recklessly foisted faulty products on an unsuspecting American society. It was hell on earth for large corporations and their insurers.

Under extreme financial pressure from corporate America,

coupled with slanted, national media attention, the Mississippi legislature revised its laws to place severe limits on the amount of money a jury can award in any given lawsuit. Nevertheless, in 1995, the laws favored plaintiffs, or at least gave them a fair shot at just reparation for their losses. So it was, when a young, African American lawyer from Jackson, Mississippi, appeared in Willie Gary's waiting room in Stuart, Florida.

Hal Dockins had met Gary at a local Mississippi Bar Association meeting, where Gary had been a guest speaker. By then Gary had secured several personal injury verdicts of more than one million dollars, bringing him limited fame among African Americans and white lawyers in the country's southeastern states. Though he previously had arranged the appointment, Gary was out of the state when Dockins arrived and not expected to return until early evening. When told this, he and his co-counsel, Mike Cavanaugh, decided to wait.

The men represented Jerry O'Keefe, along with a third attorney who chose not to attend the meeting. O'Keefe was scheduled to begin trial in several months against an international, Canadian based, funeral home conglomerate. He and the company were in litigation over a series of complex, broken agreements that resulted in him teetering on the edge of bankruptcy. O'Keefe, former mayor of Biloxi, Mississippi, and a former member of the state's legislature, is white. He was not present.

The men never did see Gary that day. They returned the following morning, again waiting several hours before finally being escorted into Gary's palatial office. Fortunately, Gary had asked me to attend the meeting, as I had examined several documents and records from the court proceedings, and it didn't take me long to get a good feel for the case. The case had been in litigation for several years. There had been a settlement agreement of that litigation which the Canadian conglomerate had breached.

Gary showed little interest in the case. His focus was on personal injury cases, as he was getting excellent settlements and verdicts. Mississippi had a particularly good statute relating to unfair trade practices and allowed punitive damages. I always had handled the more complex, commercial matters, which is why Gary invited me to the meeting in the first place. Still, he seemed to be only half listening to the men. He kept paging through his telephone messages, something he does in most meetings.

The meeting ended. Hal and Mike were walking out of the office. They looked depressed. I turned to Gary and in a voice apparently loud enough for them to hear, told him I really liked the case and we should look into it. He told me to go ahead, if I thought it was worthwhile and turned to make a telephone call. Hal Dockins recalled that event and told me, after the conclusion of the case, that he was elated on hearing my comment to Gary.

From Gary's perspective, the case presented a complicated maze of confusing facts about an utterly boring subject. He was making a small fortune handling personal injury cases, situations where one person's negligence resulted in another person being severely injured or killed. In such cases, Gary could evoke teary-eyed sympathy from jurors, while describing the agony of living in a wheel chair or children growing up without their mother's love and guidance. He could make them furious with a defendant and demand millions of dollars in reparation. Now he was being asked to talk about funeral homes and burial insurance.

The Loewen Group was headed by Ray Loewen, a Canadian businessman who had acquired over 500 funeral homes throughout his native Canada and the United States. Death is a big business. The Loewen Group was a giant in the industry and not only handled embalming and arranged burials, but marketed the caskets for huge profits and sold families burial insurance on behalf of an insurance company that also was owned by the parent corporation.

Through centralized accounting procedures and the ability to purchase everything from embalming fluids to coffins at deep, bulk-order discounts, the Canadian company was able to dramatically reduce the cost of doing business for every funeral home it acquired. Instead of passing the savings on to consumers, the company raised prices about 15 percent on average. Ray Loewen knew most families would feel guilty trying to save money on the burial of a loving mother or hard working father. He also realized that people who were suffering the loss of a loved one usually did not go shopping for funeral homes. They simply called the same place that had handled arrangements for other family members. By retaining the name of each funeral home his company purchased, often hiring the former owner as its manager, Loewen was able to take advantage of the reputation each business had built throughout its community.

I immediately had realized that such a defendant, a giant conglomerate preying upon the misery of those who just had lost loved ones, could easily be turned into the object of scorn and hatred. What potential juror who had buried a loved one, could not be made to recall the anguish of such moments and become furious with businessmen who routinely gouged people in their moment of loss. Mississippi law permitted punitive damages. Punitive damages are designed to punish egregious conduct. Who better to extract extreme punishment for such misconduct than Willie Gary? The case was tailor made for Gary.

Loewen's business tactics certainly were questionable. It was a company worth hundreds of millions of dollars, all made by taking advantage of grief stricken people on their way to church to pray for departed loved ones. At least half the jurors in Jackson would be black, with the majority being poor people barely earning a living, working menial jobs for poverty wages.

O'Keefe, on the other hand, was a popular, local businessman in his early seventies. His great-grandfather had started a funeral home business, which always had remained under family control. He had thirteen children and many of them worked in the enterprise. He was a hero in World War II and had returned home to operate his family's funeral homes. In addition to an illustrious political career, he oversaw operation of eight funeral homes throughout the state, all bearing his good family name. He also sold burial insurance and for sixteen years had enjoyed the exclusive right to sell insurance to patrons of the largest funeral home in Jackson.

In 1990, the Loewen Group had purchased the Riemann Funeral Home in Gulfport, Mississippi, from a family that had conducted the business in that community for several generations. Its success led to another acquisition of the Wright & Ferguson

Funeral Home, the company in Jackson with which O'Keefe held the contract for the exclusive sale of burial insurance. Loewen refused to honor O'Keefe's exclusive contract and immediately began selling its own insurance. O'Keefe sued to enforce his contract. In response, he received a telephone call from Ray Loewen at company headquarters in Vancouver, Canada.

By that time, Loewen had negotiated hundreds of deals acquiring funeral homes throughout North America. He had the process finely tuned and narrowed down to a science. O'Keefe was treated to the full program - a visit to the company's new corporate headquarters for meetings with the extremely personable chief executive officer, followed by a dinner cruise on the company yacht. The Alula Sprit was 110 feet long, a yacht of the Queenship class that required a full-time crew and could host as many as seventy-five partygoers. By the time the cruise up the Canadian coast was over, O'Keefe and Loewen had resolved their dispute. O'Keefe would sell three funeral homes to the Loewen Group at a price to be agreed upon later and Loewen would turn over all its insurance business in Mississippi to O'Keefe. It was an attractive arrangement for each. O'Keefe actually needed money to make up losses he suffered in a bad investment. Insurance premiums generate strong cash flow and the price for the three funeral homes was sure to be a significant addition to company coffers. Loewen simply wanted more funeral homes, having purchased over two hundred during the past two years.

O'Keefe halted progress on his lawsuit, but Loewen never stopped selling insurance. When O'Keefe again pursued the litigation, Loewen executives again contacted him to hammer out a formal agreement. O'Keefe signed it. Loewen still continued to sell insurance. There were more meetings. O'Keefe made more concessions. Months passed, and Loewen continued selling insurance. More meetings occurred and more months passed. To avoid bankruptcy, O'Keefe was forced to sell four funeral homes to another company; however, O'Keefe still faced financial disaster.

It was obvious that Loewen never intended to go through with the deal. The plan was to force Jerry O'Keefe into bankruptcy, so that Loewen could pick up his remaining funeral homes for pennies on the dollar. Hal Dockins already had amended the lawsuit to accuse Loewen of fraud and malice, and of predatory trade practices - claims that allowed punitive damages.

Dockins forwarded me boxes of material about the case, including court filed pleadings, contracts, settlement agreement, discovery materials, deposition transcripts, interrogatories and correspondence. On May 21, 1995, I sent Gary a memo that read as follows:

I have read the transcripts and reviewed the videos and relating material regarding the referred case. This is the matter referred to us by Hal Dockins from Jackson, Mississippi.

As I indicated to you, this is an excellent case and I believe we should definitely get involved. I have called Dockin's office and asked for additional material, but from what I have seen so far, this is a definite winner with a potential of a big verdict. Most of the work has been done insofar as discovery and experts, and they appeared to have done a good job. Since there is a trial certain in September that is good as well and there is sufficient time to get ready for trial, but of course, there will still be a lot of work to do. The sooner we get involved the better it will be because I do not think this is a case that can be settled, at least not before trial."

Bob P.

Gary still was not completely convinced. He grew impatient with my explanations of the facts and my projections of the possible monetary award. It was a confusing case and a far cry from the typical automobile injury case. I had trouble getting him convinced.

Finally, I told him, "Willie, if we take this case you will get the biggest verdict of your career. It will make you a true giant killer." He looked at me with wide eyes and a grin and asked with obvious pleasure, "Giant Killer?" I responded, "Yes" and then told him we must meet with O'Keefe. He enthusiastically agreed and a meeting was scheduled. So was born the name that was to follow him ever since and was used later to introduce him as a feature on the CBS television show *60 Minutes*.

The meeting took place at the Indian River Plantation, an upscale, expensive hotel and restaurant favored by many Stuart locals and visitors. We met with O'Keefe and Michael Allred, the third attorney on O'Keefe's Mississippi legal team. He had been noticeably absent from the first meeting in Gary's office and had participated little in my efforts to assemble information. Until that point, he had been the designated lead lawyer, a role he did not relish

The Giant Killers

surrendering - particularly to a black man.

It was noted that Allred definitely was a member of the Confederacy. I recall he stated that his father, or some other close relative, was a member of the Ku Klux Klan; nevertheless, he and Jerry O'Keefe had a close relationship. The meeting was cordial, but I felt Allred and Gary were quite cool toward one another.

I quickly became convinced O'Keefe was a man we wanted to represent. He was a big, likeable Irishman, who had enlisted in the Marines just a few days after Pearl Harbor. He had gone on to become the youngest Marine flying ace in the South Pacific, downing five Japanese airplanes during his assignment. As mayor of Biloxi, he once refused a parade permit for a Klan march down the main street of Biloxi.

O'Keefe and I hit it off at once. Perhaps the fact we both were World War II veterans who had seen combat was the icebreaker for us. O'Keefe had a big, beautiful family, all working in the family business. We knew there would be a twelve-person jury, at least half of whom would be black. O'Keefe would make a great impression on jurors, black or white.

As the evening progressed, Gary began to warm up to the case. I think he saw the same things in O'Keefe that I did. He also seemed to be getting a better sense of the possibilities. Finally, at one point, Gary clenched his fists and said, "I know what this case is about! Loewen lied to Jerry O'Keefe! He flat-out lied to him! This case is about lying and cheating and stealing!" When I heard that, I knew we were accepting the case. Lying, cheating and stealing became Gary's mantra thereafter and we have used it in every case since.

The theme was set, a case about "lying and cheating and stealing." That theme continued until the minute the jurors returned their verdict. Once Gary gets a handle on things, he immediately reduces them to a concept any juror can understand easily. And if Willie Gary says it is about lying, cheating and stealing, woe unto the liar, cheat and thief. Loewen would find out months down the road that he had embarked on his worst nightmare.

We signed a Contingency Fee Agreement with O'Keefe. We formed a team of lawyers and support personnel to ready the case for trial. Three months earlier, Hockins had traveled to Cincinnati to meet with Loewen lawyers in an effort to settle the case. He had demanded $6.5 million. By the time that meeting ended he was dispatched without as much as a counter offer by Loewen lawyers.

Gary announced his entry into the case with a settlement demand of his own, $125 million, roughly twenty times the demand Hockins had made three short months earlier. Loewen lawyers ignored the demand. The only indication they even received it was the appearance of a new defense attorney, Richard Sinkfield.

Sinkfield was from Atlanta, Georgia. He was an experienced courtroom combatant who specialized in complex commercial cases. He also was black, the first African American to assume a prominent role on Loewen's defense team. Perhaps his selection at that late date was coincidental.

Metropolitan areas have high minority populations. When lawsuits, particularly civil rights cases, started appearing in courts where minority jurors could be expected, some defense lawyer invariably ended up on the defense team who just happened to have the same minority status as the plaintiffs and the anticipated jurors. Cases claiming racial discrimination in areas where an appreciable number of black jurors were expected found African American attorneys at the defense table, often doing nothing but sitting there being black. This turned out not to be the case with Richard Sinkfield, as he would prove to be Gary's primary and active opponent in the courtroom.

As the trial date approached, Gary began making the rounds of African American churches in Jackson, introducing himself to the ministers and being introduced, in turn, to the congregations. He often was asked to say a few words to parishioners otherwise gathered to offer their praise to their Lord. Before the service was over, most found themselves praising Willie Gary.

By the time jury selection began, Gary was well known throughout Jackson, Mississippi's African American community. There were twelve people on that jury; eight of them were black.

I am normally a cautious man, not prone to become overly optimistic about the potential outcome of trials. By 1995, I had been practicing law for well over four decades. Before moving to Florida, I had tried lawsuits in Michigan courts for thirty years and full well knew that juries are unpredictable. I had seen many juries reject claims that were flawless. I also had seen some juries return large awards in cases that bordered on frivolity.

By the time the Loewen case started trial in Jackson, I had been participating as co-counsel with Gary, trying cases for over ten years, and had seen one remarkable, favorable verdict after another.

Time, and again, I witnessed Gary mesmerize jurors with his down to earth tactics and evangelical arguments. I also knew that lawyers from large corporate law firms were superb at blanketing their opponents in endless paperwork and actively concealing evidence in any way possible. Once trial started, however, they usually proved woefully inadequate, ill prepared and largely unlikable. They invariably were no match for our team.

I was unusually confident in the Loewen case. In my mind, it likely was a claim that would elevate my friend and partner to unthinkable heights. The facts were strong. The potential damages were immense. The defense attorneys were typical of those we had devastated in the past. I believed it was clearly a winner and the only issue was how much we would win. I was sure the amount would be staggering.

I remember our first day there. We had arranged to stay at the Waltham Hotel in downtown Jackson, just down the street from the capitol. I was having dinner in the hotel dining room when the owner came over to introduce himself. He knew Jerry O'Keefe and he had heard about the case. After we chatted a while, he asked me if I thought we had a strong case. I replied by asking him how much Dom Perignon champagne he had in his wine cellar. He said he had a couple of bottles. I told him to order a case. He did, as he reminded me later at the celebration at trial's end.

By the time trial started, as is our practice in all trials, we had familiarized ourselves with the courthouse and the courtroom where trial would be held. We had introduced ourselves to the judge's staff.

I was with Gary as we entered the courtroom and saw the

court bailiff, a portly friendly black woman. She rushed up to him, put her arms around him and made a loud gushy remark about how wonderful it was to have him in her courtroom. I glanced at the lawyers for Loewen, who were observing this remarkable scene and saw Sinkfield's eyebrows flash up to his hairline. He was just beginning to comprehend what lay ahead for him in the weeks to follow.

The trial started on September 12, 1995. The endless hours of laboring over documents and preparing witnesses were over. It finally was time for us to position ourselves at plaintiff's counsel table, the one nearest to the jury. For the next two months, we would be supporting players in the real-life drama of trial, doing our part to assist our star. It was time for Gary to go to work.

Civil and criminal juries decide issues of fact. Judges wrestle with the complex legal questions. In civil cases, like the Loewen trial, the jury would have to determine whether Jerry O'Keefe was wronged, and if so, how much money he should be awarded. The judge would instruct them about the proper law it would have to follow in reaching those decisions.

The judge was Harold Graves, a black jurist in his middle forties, who since then has been elevated to the Appellate Court. He would know of Gary's background and his legal abilities in the courtroom. His judicial assistant was an attractive black girl in her thirties and it didn't take long for Gary to develop a close relationship with her, which proved to be of immeasurable value as the trial went on.

Some judges insist upon doing all the questioning in jury

selection, using questions submitted in advance by the lawyers. These judges reason that this practice prevents any lawyer from influencing jurors by direct, verbal contact; however, Judge Graves permitted Gary and his adversary, Richard Sinkfield, to ask the questions; therefore, Gary had his first chance to talk with the jurors. He went right to work when introducing himself and his client to the potential decision makers. The trial transcript reads:

MR. GARY: "My name is Willie Gary. I come from a little farming town down in south Florida called Indiantown, and I came to Jackson with my partners, Lorenzo Williams, who is over here, and Robert Parenti. We teamed up with our good friends, Mike Allred, Hal Dockins and Mike Cavanaugh, to represent one of your own, Jerry O'Keefe and his family. Jerry, I want you to stand so they can see you. And then I want your children to stand because they are part of this too. Jeff, where are you? Can you all see Jeff? Jeff. We have Betty in here. Will you stand? Susan, will you stand? Catherine, okay. That's the O'Keefe family along with some others that you will get a chance to meet later throughout the course of this case."

That is so typical Willie. He tells the jurors he is from a little farming town. He might just as well have said, "Just like you folks," or "We are just alike." Then he introduces Lorenzo and me as his partners, so we must be like the jurors too. He talks about teaming up with "good friends," like we all went to school together. In seconds, he is making it a personal case with

O'Keefe and his family, telling jurors Jerry is "one of your own" and introducing family members as if we were all close neighbors who were going to sit down for dinner together.

Sinkfield just sat there, along with his co-counsel with a professional smile on his face. I glanced at him and thought to myself, "I think he is beginning to realize what he is in for." The transcript continued:

MR. GARY: "Do you all believe in the jury system? Do you believe in the jury system? You've got to tell me now. This is the only time I get a chance to talk to you. You've either got to nod with me or raise your hands. And you all believe in what the jury system stands for in America? Do you feel that every man or woman, boy or girl should have the right to come to court and have a jury of his or her peers decide their case? Do all of you agree with that?"

In seconds, Gary had every possible juror in that room committing to the jury system. He had all of them making a personal promise to him, not to the judge and not to all the other lawyers, just to him, that they were committed not only to the jury system, but to Willie Gary. The transcript continued:

MR. GARY: "So now, you know, members of the jury, I have a big - not big mouth, but a loud voice anyway, so if during the course of this trial, would you promise me one thing? If I do talk loud, and I get a little fiery sometime, I do. But would you promise me one thing, all of you, that if that happens and you think I'm talking too loud or yelling or you may not like the suit I'm wearing, whatever, you won't hold that against me? You can take it out on me, but don't take it out on my client. Will you promise to do that?"

MR. SINKFIELD: "Your Honor, objection, please."

JUDGE GRAVES: "State it."

MR. SINKFIELD: "Commitment, Your Honor. He can ask if they have a feeling about the case, but not for a commitment."

JUDGE GRAVES: "Overruled."

Sinkfield knew something was wrong. Things already were not going well for him and we had only been in the courtroom for a few minutes. The trial had not even started yet.

MR. GARY: "Now I say that, because members of the jury let me give you some idea of what you are involved with in this case. There will be claims as high as $650 million to $850 million. I want you to look me in the face and tell me now if that's going to bother anybody in here. If it's going to cause any problems to anybody here in sitting and making a fair and impartial decision, let me see your hands right now. All right. I want you to be honest with us. That's what I want is you to be honest with us."

I had seen Gary do that many times in past trials. He was telling the prospective jurors before even being selected that he wanted hundreds of millions of dollars and, in essence, getting them to make an early commitment that they just might be willing to give it to him, that they agreed that could be a fair and impartial verdict.

Sinkfield just sat there. I knew he realized Gary was putting something over on him and on the jurors, but he was not quite able to figure out how to verbalize his objections so he could ask the Judge to stop him. Gary just kept on going.
The transcript:

MR. GARY: "Have you ever experienced a situation or do you know anyone who ever experienced a situation where you made a deal with someone else, and then he tried to renege on it based on technicalities? Has anybody ever done that? Now would you raise your hand for me please? Do any of you, now Mr. Watson (one of the prospective jurors) could you do that?"

Gary was on a roll. From the very beginning, he was making it his case, to be tried by his rules, with his jurors. Sinkfield was sinking and there was hardly any water in the pool yet. Gary knew that and took full advantage of it.

MR. GARY: "Let me say this. Ray Loewen is not - that group is from Canada and I remember that question you had on the questionnaire about you've got to give anybody a fair trial. Just because the group is from Canada, you still have to give them a fair trial.. Do you all agree with that? I want to make that clear, but you will also agree that if they come down to Mississippi to do business in Mississippi, they've got to play by the same rules. You all agree with that? One set of rules right?"

MR. SINKFIELD: "Your Honor, I'm going to object again. I hate to interrupt the flow of this, but every question seeks a commitment. He can ask them if they have feelings if people in other places should be treated differently, but the repeated affirmation is a violation of our rules."

JUDGE GRAVES: "Overruled."

By that point, it didn't matter how the Judge ruled, though denying the objection sure didn't help Sinkfield any. It was the local Judge telling the local jury that their small town visitor from another small town in the Deep South was right and the slick, big city lawyer from up in Atlanta was out of line.

By the time Gary was finished with his questions he had the jurors prepared to watch a real drama unfold before their very eyes. They were going to hear about a monstrous, foreign company coming to town to make a deal with a small, local businessman and then try backing out on the basis of technicalities. They were going to learn exactly how that company had broken their rules, the same rules that apply to every man and woman, and every boy and girl, in Mississippi. Finally, Gary would tell them how many hundreds of millions of dollars they should award.

There were twelve people on the jury that finally were selected, eight African Americans and four whites. Gary set about pursuing the simplistic theme he had hit upon at dinner, just a few months earlier at the Indian River Plantation; a case of lying, cheating and stealing, rather than a complicated situation involving questions of numerous documents and what they might or might not mean - technically speaking. He clearly planned to make it a matter of David versus Goliath, and David would be played by Jerry O'Keefe, a small, local businessman with a beautiful, loving family.

Gary left nothing to chance. He insisted that O'Keefe's wife of more than fifty years, Annette, remain seated next to her husband throughout the arduous trial. She was a tiny portly woman who easily could be pictured in her apron baking apple pies and dishing sumptuous meals to her burgeoning family. Each day of trial would find at least a half dozen O'Keefe children dressed in their best Sunday suits, seated dutifully in the first row of the spectators' section behind their parents.

Prior to starting the trial and picking the jury, Gary had arranged to have a family picture made of O'Keefe and his wife in the center with all of the children and grandchildren seated around him in a nice outdoor setting by their home. The picture was enormous, probably twelve feet wide by four feet high and Gary had convinced the judge, over strenuous objection from Loewen's lawyers, that it should be a trial exhibit, because all of the family members worked in the family funeral home and it was legally appropriate. He was able to keep the portrait leaned up against the jury rail during the entire trial. The defense had to stare at it throughout trial. Of course, they were unhappy about it because the jury and every witness that testified would be looking at it. But The photograph simply was too much for Sinkfield and his array of corporate lawyers. He immediately objected to the picture, stating, "The only purpose for which this kind of exhibition is being offered is to try to incur sympathy and favor out of the jury," he complained to Judge Graves. The Judge listened. The picture stayed. And There it sat for nearly two months.

Sinkfield was helpless to do anything about the family attending trial. Courtrooms are public forums, open for all interested citizens and Gary was making it clear that the O'Keefe family was intensely interested in what would go on during the trial, standing squarely behind their mom and dad at every step of the proceedings.

Opening statements by the lawyers followed the jury selection. These are opportunities for the lawyers to tell jurors what they expect to show during an upcoming trial. They are not, however, designed to permit attorneys an early chance to argue their case. A lawyer is simply supposed to highlight the anticipated testimony, and perhaps show jurors the exhibits to be utilized during the trial. The idea is for the jurors to learn in advance what the case is all about and how each lawyer intends to establish his position. It is merely intended as an outline for the jury to follow during trial.

Numerous studies show that when presented with new material or meeting new people, most humans form firm and lasting impressions quite quickly. When meeting a stranger, we tend to decide while shaking his hand whether we like or dislike him. When starting a new book, we tend to decide if we are going to enjoy it before finishing the first chapter. Trial experts recognize the importance of this trait, realizing that jurors, and even judges, tend to decide how they will resolve a dispute on the basis of first impressions. They will tend to pay close attention to any evidence that supports their early decision and disregard evidence that suggests they may have been mistaken.

There are books abound offering attorneys advice about how to make the most of opening statements. Few, if any lawyers, realize this more readily than Willie Gary. While his questioning of jurors obviously was designed to make favorable first impressions of him, his client and his case, his opening statement would go even further. He told jurors the case involved, "the oldest sin known to anybody, and that's greed." He described O'Keefe as a man, "of family values," saying he was one who "would fight for what's right and what he believes in." Each time he would refer to O'Keefe, Gary would walk to where his client was sitting and place a hand on his shoulder.

Those jurors left court each day knowing that Gary had become attached to O'Keefe. It sure was not lost on the African American jurors, that black hand resting on O'Keefe's shoulder reassuringly. I think the white jurors were equally impressed. They all liked Gary, and O'Keefe was Gary's friend; therefore, O'Keefe had to be a good guy.

Sinkfield, together with two additional blacks - both local, one of whom was a state representative; and a distinguished white lawyer, a former Supreme Court justice, continued to be overwhelmed by our juggernaut. Sinkfield, in his opening statement, portrayed himself as an urbane country gentleman, as he was. He wore a vest together with a dark suit, throughout the entire trial. In his opening statement, he commented to the jury that his mother always believed he should wear a vest because it exuded some sort of respectability. As distinguished and respectable as he was, the jury appeared more impressed with Gary.

Just as Gary made it clear how he felt about O'Keefe, he made it abundantly clear what he thought of Ray Loewen, describing him as one who "wouldn't keep his word, deceived people and would not deal with honor." He described Loewen, who actually stayed away from court throughout most of the trial, as a man who tried "to dominate markets, create monopolies and gouge families that are grieving."

Gary was trying the case against an empty chair. I don't know what Ray Loewen thought was going on in Jackson, but it was clear to the jury that he did not seem to care very much. Staying away from the trial was just the same as telling the jury he didn't care what they did; he was just too busy to be bothered with them.

As far as the facts were concerned, no one doubted that O'Keefe had a contract for the exclusive right to sell burial insurance through Wright & Ferguson, or that he had enjoyed the benefits of that right for more than 16 years. There also was no doubt that the Loewen Group had negotiated and signed an agreement designed to resolve its dispute with O'Keefe over the loss of those rights, though Loewen lawyers tried arguing that their client never breached the contract in the first place.

"Didn't breach the contract?" Gary asked one defense witness. "Well, why did you come to Mississippi to sign a settlement agreement if you haven't breached the contract?" There was no answer available that sounded anything less than downright silly.

Gary pounded home the fact that the company went on to breach the agreement they entered to cure the harm done by its breach of the first contract, essentially breaching contract after contract. Loewen attorneys replied that the second agreement really was not an agreement at all. They claimed it was just "an agreement to agree." Gary had them claiming the company entered an agreement to resolve its breach of a contract it never breached, and failed to adhere to the written agreement because it really was not an agreement at all, but just an agreement to agree. If the jury was confused, rather than amused, Gary would explain it all quite simply during his closing argument:

MR. GARY: "They wanted Jerry out of business. They used that settlement agreement to dangle in front of him. They started coming up with all these excuses, one after another, one after another, one after another and, poor man, he made one concession after another. They beat him down, seventy-two years old, they beat him down, they beat him and they beat him, and it's not right."

That made a lot more sense to the jury than what Loewen lawyers were trying to peddle. The jury was offended, plain and simple. They were offended that the company would treat one of their own like that and they were offended that the lawyers would try selling them such nonsense. Gary would convince them that the company treated Jerry O'Keefe like a backwoods hick and its lawyers were treating them like backwoods hicks.

Corporate greed is a powerful tool and Gary took full advantage of it throughout the trial. The proof produced at trial showed the jury how Loewen would gouge bereaved families over the price of coffins. One supplier sold Loewen a particularly attractive model of coffins for $940 each, which included shipping costs. The company charged $2,860 to families in Corinth, Mississippi, 200 miles from Jackson, Mississippi, where there was little or no competition. In Jackson, however, where it faced meaningful competition, it sold the same coffin for $1,920.

"Some poor fellow has to pay a thousand dollars more for just a box? Just a box?" Gary would tell the jury later. "They are just shipped out by the people who make them; funeral home doesn't even have to touch it, doesn't have to put it in the hearse, doesn't have to shovel one bit of dirt. They charge $2,860, that's almost $2,000 for making the phone call! That ain't right! Talking about a monopoly, deceptive trade practices!"

That relentless theme of corporate greed would continue.

VI

THE VERDICT
ONE VOTE SHORT

Winning multimillion-dollar verdicts had become easy
for Willie Gary, and he began to want something bigger.
JONATHAN HARR, the New Yorker Magazine
"The Burial" November 1, 1999

L oewen lawyers scrambled to try explaining away one incident after another of the company's efforts to dominate the markets where it did business, and its common practice of increasing consumer prices at every funeral home it acquired. There may well have been an arguable position, that Loewen had not breached O'Keefe's contract with the previous owner, but we clearly intended to overwhelm that position with the description of the O'Keefe family as victims of greed. Jurors were shown a memo from one Loewen officer that discussed beating O'Keefe to Jackson, Mississippi's burial insurance customers and stating, "I believe we would easily dominate the market." We called the company's former Mississippi controller as a witness. She had participated in several of its acquisitions. She said she resigned because of the company's ongoing practice of increasing the fees to its customers.

John Wright, with whom O'Keefe had made the contract

for the Wright & Ferguson insurance business in Jackson, testified that he had remained with Loewen after selling his company to the Loewen Group. He acknowledged that the company had often raised prices for its services without consulting him, though his family had been serving as undertakers in the Jackson community for several decades.

In his blistering opening statement, Gary had mentioned the Alula Spirit, telling jurors it was, "a yacht that the company spends a million dollars a year just to keep." It was not something upon which he intended to dwell during trial, though he felt it worth mentioning as part of his reference to corporate greed. Sinkfield and his team obviously were concerned about reference to the yacht; however, they kept bringing it up, apparently thinking it was something they had to explain. It was worth Gary mentioning it in his opening, but we were far less interested in it than the damning evidence we were presenting about how this company did business. It was a typical overreaction by corporate attorneys. They were afraid of it, so they blew it up into something far more damaging to their own case than it otherwise would have been. It started with testimony from a friendly Loewen executive under examination by one of the company's own lawyers, who asked if the company had a boat. The executive denied the company owned the craft, saying, "from time to time we rent a boat." The attorney pursued the issue.

Q: "Who owns the boat you rent?"

A: "The boat is owned by a private company which, in turn, is owned by Mr. Raymond Loewen. We rent it on a daily basis, to insure that it's available on short notice. We pay what's called a standby fee."

The questioning went on to closely examine how the company felt the yacht was useful for doing business and how the board of directors which, of course, was controlled by Raymond Loewen, set the rental fees.

They were doing our work for us. They were telling this jury from a poor Mississippi community how Ray Loewen owns this huge boat, how his company rents it from him, paying for it every day at a rate set by Raymond Loewen's hand-picked board of directors.

Whether Judge Graves simply wanted to move the trial along or whether he felt the lawyers were doing too much damage to their own client, likely will never be known, but he tried to intercede the following morning. He warned the lawyers at a bench conference that he wanted no further testimony about the boat stating, "They spent a whole hour yesterday trying to explain that we don't have a big yacht, but we do. I'm so sick of hearing about that. I'm the only person in here without a boat, and I've got to hear about these dinner cruises."

Judge Graves is a fair man. He really wanted the parties to stick to the issues and I believe what he was really saying is that the jury was sick of hearing about the thing and warning the defense attorneys that, if he did not have a boat, those jurors did not either. They just could not let the thing go. They brought it up again when

Ray Loewen was testifying. It was obvious that even Loewen did not know why they were doing it, and he wasn't even prepared. The transcript of Loewen's testimony reads as follows (Direct Examination by Sinkfield):

Q: "You mentioned dinner cruises. Is that a boat or is that a yacht?"

A: "I really don't know the difference."

Q: "It's a big boat, isn't it?"

A: "I don't know what's big, but it is 110 feet long. I'm not sure if that is big."

It was just too much for Gary to pass up. I could see him twisting around in his chair when all those verbal gymnastics were going on. I could not wait for his cross examination of Loewen and I wasn't disappointed.

The transcript of Loewen's testimony reads (Cross Examination by Gary):

Q: "Let me ask you this. Does your board of directors know that you don't know the difference between a boat and a yacht?"

A: "I've had the privilege of entertaining my directors on my boat."

Q: "Do they know that you don't know the difference between a boat and a yacht?"

A: "I doubt if they know that."

Q: "Can you land a helicopter on your canoe, boat, yacht, whichever one?"

A: "My helicopter pilot can land a helicopter on my boat."

Q: "Oh, you've got your own helicopter and your pilot?"

A: "Yes."

Some of the jurors looked dumbfounded. These were people who sometimes had trouble making the payments on their old trucks; meanwhile, here is this wealthy CEO sitting up there trying to spar with Gary while talking about his 110-foot boat, and how his helicopter pilot can land his helicopter on it.

The defense attorneys simply were never in touch with that jury. I never have understood why big companies insist on using lawyers who are accustomed to working with huge dollar figures and who have absolutely no empathy with the typical "man on the street." Jurors are selected from "men on the street," not corporate executives. Business practices that are commonplace in corporate boardrooms are as foreign to most people as the Chinese language.

Our opponents were trying to explain big yachts and multi-million dollar dealings as if they happen every day in everybody's life. Those jurors were simple people who were used to spending every day of their lives worrying about mortgages, credit card payments and college tuition for their kids. The cavalier approach those lawyers took to money issues was just downright offensive. They were destined to be punished. Their client was going to be punished. I just knew that was going to happen the first day I heard about the case in Gary's office.

"The defense team," Judge Graves remarked later, "never had any idea how out-of-touch they were with what was going on."

The media covered the trial on a daily basis. At the close of each day, reporters and TV cameras were waiting in the courthouse corridors. Gary has a particular attraction to the press. It became a common sight that, when everyone would walk out of the courtroom, the reporters would rush up to Gary with pen and pad in hand to get his comments and trample the rest of us in the stampede. Attractive female reporters seem to enjoy his personality and repartee and Gary never fails to accommodate them, frequently hugging them, sometimes with an accompanying kiss, as if they were longtime friends or family.

On one particular day, Gary had left the courtroom earlier and I had stood in for him and argued a difficult legal question before the judge. When the session ended, I walked out into the courtroom and there, as usual, was Gary surrounded by the reporters. I waited for the interview to end and then Gary and I together walked alone back to the hotel, a few blocks away. Out of frustration from the day that

I had had in the courtroom, I began to complain and ask him, "Why is it that the reporters always rush up to you and they never ask my opinions on anything about the court proceedings, even though I am actively involved?" Gary looked at me with that big grin of his, that has now become a trademark, and said "Bob, no one is interested in you."

There certainly was no ill will intended by that remark and we both laughed, but it struck me at the time, and it does to this day, that it certainly had a degree of truth in it. I told that story later that evening, when the lawyers met at the hotel bar, as usual. They all laughed and joked about it, but they also consoled me and agreed that it was just "Willie's way." I had another drink and left the bar in mock humility, hanging my head and retired to prepare for the next day.

After two months of trial, the case was approaching its climatic end. We began to plan the preparation of our final arguments to the jury. My confidence had increased as the case proceeded and I felt assured that we would obtain a verdict and substantial money damages.

Hal Dockins and I commenced working on the proposed jury instructions, which each side prepares and presents to the judge, prior to submission of the case to the jury. The judge then determines which instructions are applicable and instructs the jury, after both sides have concluded their case, as to which law they must apply in arriving at a verdict. This case was relatively straight forward, essentially involving breaches of contract and monopolistic practices, coupled with unfair trade practices. If the jury found that there was a violation of the laws by the defendant as the judge instructed them, they were to award monetary damages, to Jerry O'Keefe and his company.

Lorenzo Williams and I worked with Gary throughout the night before the anticipated day for our final argument. We had little or no sleep but greeted the dawn with anticipation and confidence.

We walked together to the courthouse, briefcases in hand, and wandered through the groups standing outside of the courthouse awaiting the end of the drama that could well prove to be the case of the century. Up until that time, the largest verdict rendered by a jury in Mississippi was $18 million. The press, of course, surrounded us and national media was there with their TV cameras. The courtroom was full, with standing room only, and the bailiff kept the doors closed as the proceedings commenced.

Gary was brilliant, as usual, and had the jury nodding at every word he said. Loewen sat at the defendant's table with his wife, practically the only time he was in the courtroom, other than when he testified on the stand. The way the courtroom was arranged, Gary's back was to Loewen as he was addressing the jury; however, when Gary would direct some of his most caustic remarks about Loewen, he would turn directly towards him when speaking of his conduct. Loewen would only glare at him, obviously uncomfortable.

The jury was attentive to every word that Gary said. The Alula Spirit became an important basis for his theme. Gary told the jury: "These people just lied, lied, lied, lied. They lied to Jerry and they lied to you. They even lied for no reason. They lie. What about the boat? Nothing wrong with the man having a yacht, but if you've got a yacht, say it."

In almost the same breath, Gary moved on to the company's business practices stating, "If you really want to gouge someone, you catch them during that time when they've lost a mother or a father or a child. They are helpless. They are helpless. They are there for the picking. Take them. Take them. It's all about dollars with them." The lawyers for Loewen gave a tepid and typical response. Their only hope was to keep the damage award at a minimum.

The judge gave the jury its instructions and they retired to the jury room to deliberate their verdict. For most courtroom lawyers, myself included, that is a most difficult time, waiting for a jury to return a verdict. After a couple of hours, a surprisingly short time considering the complexities of the case, the jury knocked on the door. The bailiff entered the jury room and then returned with the announcement that the jury had reached a verdict.

We watched closely as the jurors filed solemnly into the courtroom. Many lawyers believe they can read a juror's face and know what the verdict is. I have never been able to do that and I generally refuse to look at them when they return to the courtroom.

When the judge asked them if they had reached their verdict, the foreman replied they had and handed the verdict form to the judge. The verdict form was lengthy. There were ten questions asked of the jury and when the judge read to us the answer to the first question, as being "yes," I glanced at Gary and he at me, with a recognized inner smile of "we won again." I glanced at Loewen after the first "yes" and he turned pale. The nine questions that followed also were answered in the affirmative, with dollar amounts attached to each answer and as it progressed, I watched Loewen. A reporter described his condition, as the verdict was read, as stupefied, with the glazed eyes and pallor of a man in the near clinical state of shock. The jury had awarded O'Keefe a total of $260 million.

Judge Graves had told the jury that any damage award was to be for whatever actual losses O'Keefe had suffered. After receiving the verdict, he told jurors they would have to return the following day to consider whether punitive damages should be awarded. The jurors were confused. They returned to their deliberation room and forwarded a note to the judge explaining that their initial award was intended to include punitive damages. They had awarded an extra one hundred million to cover such damages.

When Judge Graves told all the lawyers about the jury's note the next morning in chambers, Loewen lawyers demanded a mistrial. That would have resulted in the verdict being disregarded and trial starting all over again with a new jury. They claimed that the verdict was contrary to the evidence and the note clearly indicated that the jurors had failed to follow the judge's instructions. The judge denied their request. Instead, he proposed to allow the verdict to stand and dispense with the hearing on punitive damages, a hearing which would allow our team an opportunity to show the Loewen Company's immense net worth.

The jurors never had been told how much the company was worth. It would have been improper and prejudicial to tell them that before they even decided if there was a basis for any damages at all. Had they been told that during the trial they might have been influenced to overlook the issues altogether, since the company had so much money anyway. First they had to decide if there was any basis for O'Keefe's claim and, if so, whether he suffered any actual loss. Punitive damages were an entirely separate question.

We agreed to the judge's proposal, but only if Loewen lawyers would agree not to appeal the verdict. Loewen's lawyers asked for time, left the judge's chambers and presumably called Loewen who had left the city. They returned shortly and said our offer was rejected. The judge was incredulous. The judge said to the defense lawyers, "This note makes it clear they're going to award a hundred million dollars in compensatory damages. If I go back in there, I'm also going to allow the plaintiffs to put on evidence of net worth. I don't think you want to go back in there. You already know they've given $160 million without knowing net worth."

We had prepared to ask for punitive damages after showing the jury how much money the company had. Punitive damages only are awarded when a jury decides that the defendant's conduct is particularly offensive. They are designed to punish the defendant for such conduct and to serve as a warning to others that such conduct can produce painful results.

We spent much of the previous night with Gary discussing how much he should ask of the jury for punitive damages. He tells this story of the events: "Bob spent the night teaching me how to say one billion dollars.   Everybody else was talking about a couple of hundred million, but not Mr. P. He kept saying, 'Willie, Loewen is a multi-billion dollar conglomerate. That jury will give you just about anything you want. He talked me into the case in the first place. I had to figure he knew what he was talking about."

We had enlisted two prominent economists to testify about the net worth of the Loewen Company. They both agreed that it exceeded $3 billion. Of course, Loewen lawyers had their own experts as well.

We had previously spent hours with our experts making sure their testimony was well reasoned and well coordinated. Sinkfield asserted in his presentation to the jury that the Loewen Group had a net worth of only $411 million; however, the economist called to testify on Loewen's behalf stated that, in his opinion, the company was worth between six and seven hundred million dollars. It became obvious Loewen lawyers had been less thorough.

For Loewen, this was by any measure, a grievous example of a poorly coordinated presentation by his legal team. But Loewen wasn't there that day to witness it. He had already left town, unable to face the ordeal of sitting once again in the courtroom.

Gary did indeed have a field day when it came time for him to make his closing argument on the punitive damage issue stating:

MR. GARY: "Members of the jury, they came in here even this morning trying to weasel and slip and slide. The net worth of this company went from $411 million to almost $700 million in less than thirty minutes. That's what we've been dealing with," reminding jurors the company owned 800 funeral homes and 172 cemeteries. You think Ray Loewen would sell all of that business, all of those companies, for $411 million?"

Regarding the owner's absence that day, Gary said, "He

didn't even show up today. That's the ultimate arrogance." When it came to money, Gary's voice rose to the crescendo of the finest preacher in the finest pulpit as he said, "One billion dollars, ladies and gentlemen of the jury. One billion dollars."

When the crowd heard that, there was some stir among the spectators in the courtroom. I glanced at Lorenzo and he did to me, with both of our eyebrows raised. It did not cause any emotion among the jurors, but prior to that statement the jurors were frequently nodding their head at whatever Gary said. It was quite obvious there was going to be a substantial verdict.

Less than an hour passed before the jury returned an award of $400 million, bringing its verdict to a grand total of a half billion dollars.

(Top Left) Robert Parenti, Madison McClellan
Johnnie Cochran, Willie Gary

The judge recessed the court and we spilled out into the corridors to the waiting crowd of reporters, cameras and friends. Everyone was euphoric - laughing and slapping each other on the back, hugging and kissing, at least on our side. The interviews lasted perhaps an hour and then the crowd retired to the hotel banquet room, where the Dom Perignom, promised months before by the hotel's owner, was awaiting us in chilled silver ice buckets, with accompanying hors d'oeuvres.

We eagerly awaited the evening news reports and we were

not disappointed on what we saw and heard. Gary was shown on the full screen with Jerry O'Keefe hugging, smiling and laughing, with Gary's grin covering most of the screen. After five minutes or so of coverage, Gary shouted across the room, "Hey Bob, I see you. Look." Sure enough, tucked away in the lower corner of the screen the back of my head, clearly balding, was visible. "Yes I see it," I said and I hung my head again in mock humility.

The victory party continued the next morning at Mary Mahoney's Old French House Restaurant in Biloxi. The restaurant is well known and not far from Jerry's house, which stood on the main thoroughfare overlooking the Gulf of Mexico. The party was in the garden of the famous restaurant. There was a microphone set up and accompanying music. Everyone of note spoke at the party. All of the family members giving their stories, thanking the lawyers. I said a few words comparing the battle in the courtroom to my war experience during the Battle of the Bulge. Susan O'Keefe, Jerry's daughter, thanked me for recommending the case. The highlight of the evening was Willie taking over the microphone and singing his theme song, "Stand by Me." He realized that he was then probably, the most famous lawyer in the United States, if not the world. He had just won a $500 million jury verdict, the largest of its kind in the history of American jurisprudence.

I was told later that in that celebration crowd were two of the jurors, although I was not aware of it at the time. I was also told that a juror had stated that the jury had been just one vote short of awarding the billion dollars that Gary had demanded.

VII

IT'S NOT OVER - 'TIL-

I'm just thankful for the jury verdict that
makes everybody play by the rules.
Jerry O'Keefe, Sr.

The actual judgment for $500 million was signed by Judge Graves on November 6, 1995. Some observers believed it was the largest single jury verdict in America. The sheer magnitude of such an award made headlines throughout the nation. A *Wall Street Journal* headline read, "A Small Canadian Firm Meets the American Tort Monster." *Time* magazine featured the story in its next edition. National television networks promptly reported it among their lead stories.

Needless to say, Willie Gary's name played a prominent role in nearly all the stories, some emphasizing his rise from a poor, itinerant farming family and highlighting his history of numerous, multi-million dollar verdicts. Several years later, Jonathan Harr, author of the best selling book *A Civil Action*, would publish a lengthy article about the Loewen case in *The New Yorker* magazine, and it would serve as the introduction of a feature on Gary by the popular television news magazine, *60 Minutes*.

Despite all the publicity, the case was not yet finished. Headlines tell of large verdicts. Seldom does the media follow up to report how such cases finally conclude. Nearly every such verdict ends up in settlement for a much smaller sum or appellate courts often reduce them or set them aside all together.

This well serves corporate America and its insurance companies. They repeatedly publicize such verdicts as part of their ongoing, public relations efforts to convince Americans that the jury system is out of control. Whenever insurance companies suffer losses resulting from their poor investment practices, they impose outrageous premium increases on their policyholders. If questioned about this practice, they divert attention to courtroom lawyers and huge verdicts, claiming they are rendered helpless as long as the laws permit jurors to operate unchecked.

The Loewen case was no exception to the rule. Within days, company lawyers were seeking relief from Judge Graves, just as conservative media giants were heralding it as, yet another example how the jury system was endangering our American way of life.

Once the euphoria wore off, we knew the case had to be settled. If not, it would be tied up in the appellate courts for years and most likely would be reduced. Worse yet, it could be set aside altogether. Meanwhile, our seventy-two-year-old client probably would never live to see a penny. That judgment was just a piece of paper. We would reap the publicity benefits, but Jerry O'Keefe would go to his grave with nothing more than a sense of satisfaction and a lot of frustration. He would have gone through all that and have nothing to show for it.

The Loewen Group's attorney first appealed to Judge Graves, filing documents seeking a new trial, outright reversal of the judgment, or a reduction in the award. The judge heard arguments on their requests just fourteen days after signing the judgment. He denied them all. If Loewen wanted relief, however, he would have to get it from the Mississippi Supreme Court.

One day after the judgment had been signed, attorneys from both sides met in a New Orleans hotel to explore settlement possibilities. Willie, Lorenzo and I attended on O'Keefe's behalf.

Loewen's lawyers acted as if they were in a coma. True to form, they refused to be realistic. They proposed full settlement for less than $20 million. They were acting as if they had won the case. There was a whole lot of shouting. When we finally walked out, there was $25 million on the table.

The potential downside was not lost on O'Keefe. We had fully informed him of the perils that lie ahead and, being a sensible businessman, he wanted closure. Loewen common stock was crashing. Investment houses with a large stake in the company were calling him to beg for mercy. At a hearing with Judge Graves, after the jurist had denied all defense requests, we demanded a cash bond to secure his judgment.

Appeal bonds are designed to insure that defendants do not dispose of their assets while lengthy appeals drag on through the courts. In Mississippi, the law required a cash bond equal to 125 percent of the verdict. The state's legislature had reasoned that interest would run on awards under appeal and the amount of a bond should be high enough to comfortably insure there would be enough cash on hand to pay the full amount if the appeal failed. We had analyzed Loewen's assets for use in the hearing on punitive damages. We knew that the company likely would be unable to come up with that much money without crippling its entire operation. Judge Graves granted our request; more than likely guessing that such a ruling would seriously encourage the defense to reach a settlement. If the case settled, any appeal would be abandoned. His decision could not be reversed, something loathed by trial judges everywhere in the country.

Loewen Company lawyers then sought relief from the Mississippi Supreme Court, asking that the bond be reduced to $125 million. That court refused to interfere. The bond would stand. We were right. Ray Loewen could not post such a bond without destroying his credit lines and stifling, if not destroying, his entire empire. The Supreme Court had given the company seven days to post the bond. Failure would allow us to start seizing Loewen assets. Jonathan Harr would later write:

> By now, Loewen had begun to suspect that he was the victim of a conspiracy. In time, this suspicion grew to an absolute conviction. He could never adduce the proof to support a conspiracy, yet he saw coincidence and dark synchronicity everywhere. Among other things, he had read a novel by John Grisham called *The Runaway Jury*, about a fictional lawsuit tried in Biloxi, of all places, in which a juror conspires to deliver a huge verdict. The truth about his own case, he came to believe, was a conspiracy broader and more twisted than even this fiction. He could not conceive that his circumstances might be the product of his own making, or even just a matter of bad luck.

One day after the Supreme Court ruling, we wrote Loewen's lawyers: "Please be advised that as of 12 noon, Wednesday, January 31, 1996, we shall start execution on all property, real and personal, that you have in the state of Mississippi and in other states as well." We gave them one last chance to settle the case, demanding $475 million.

Loewen wanted to settle. O'Keefe wanted to settle. A Loewen executive, Larry Miller, called O'Keefe directly, offering to sit down and try resolving the case. Miller suggested meeting at the Ritz-Carlton Hotel in Atlanta, Georgia, the following day. O'Keefe agreed. He flew there with Allred, meeting Gary, Williams, and me at the hotel. Miller opened the meeting with a $50 million counter offer to settle everything. The meeting lasted from late morning through the entire night with each side hurling accusations and threats, then breaking to caucus and returning for renewed posturing.

O'Keefe wanted to settle the thing. He looked exhausted. The years of uncertainty had taken a terrible toll on him and his family and he longed to return to Biloxi with the whole experience behind him. The $50 million looked awfully good to him. He wanted us to accept it. We just had to keep O'Keefe under control. As it turned out, he not only remained under control, he broke the impasse.

In our final session, O'Keefe made a businessman's proposal. He would accept the $50 million in cash. He realized the problems Loewen would face if pushed much further and knew that if it were him, he would head for the safety of a bankruptcy court. He had every reason to believe Loewen would do the same thing, so he accepted the $50 million as a down payment, together with a million shares of Loewen stock at a guaranteed price of thirty dollars per share. He also demanded a non-interest bearing note for an additional $200 million, payable over the next twenty years.

The proposal was accepted and settlement agreements were prepared and executed. Like most things in life, especially where lawyers are involved, there never seems to be an end to some experiences and there was more to come here as well.

Ray Loewen kept on doing business as if nothing had happened. He threw the company into a financial shambles before the stockholders finally threw him out as chief executive officer. By then it was too late. In 1999, the stock dropped to fifty-three cents a share and the company went bankrupt. Its stock was worthless.

Experienced lawyers realize that cases often are not over, even after the money has been paid. In fact, the money itself often gives rise to an entirely new wave of problems. The Loewen case was over as far as O'Keefe was concerned. To commemorate its conclusion, he had the hundreds of pages of settlement documents bound in a rich, green leather binder. It resembles law books found in most attorneys' offices and bears the case title on the spine on a black background, "Jeremiah J. O'Keefe, Sr., et al. Vs. The Loewen Group, Inc., et al. He sent a copy to me with a handwritten note inscribed on the front page dated Dec. 4, 1996. It read as follows: "Bob. Please keep this as a memento of this historic case. We want you to know how much we appreciate the effort you put into this to make it so successful."

The post judgment maneuvering was not limited to the O'Keefe attorneys. The Loewen Company filed for bankruptcy.

While that proceeding was pending, Loewen filed a claim against the United States government, employing a provision of the National Fair Trade Agreement (NAFTA), to seek reimbursement of its losses from American taxpayers.

NAFTA had been adopted shortly after William Jefferson Clinton became president. It was supported by every living former president of the United States and was vehemently opposed by American labor unions, which continues to hold true today. Its purpose is to encourage the free flow of commerce among various, North American countries. Unions complained it would cost thousands of American jobs by making it easier for American companies to open factories in foreign nations where labor costs are a fraction of those in America. Mexican workers would work for a few dollars a day, as opposed their American counterparts who often are paid more than twenty dollars an hour. The affect of the treaty on the economy of the country continues to be a political battleground.

The law contains a logical provision that a foreign company should be protected from unfair treatment by the government of the host company. The Loewen Company claimed that Gary's closing argument during trial was an unfair characterization of the facts, thus constituting a violation of the Treaty that entitled the company to reimbursement of at least some of the money lost in trial. In essence, it was a back door attempt to obtain a determination that the American judicial system is unfair and any foreign company that suffers a loss in American courts might be able to recover those losses from our government through NAFTA.

The official proceeding was commenced in the International

Centre for Settlement of Investment Disputes in Washington, D.C., before a three-judge tribunal of international judges, as provided by the Treaty - one representing each country, namely United States, Canada and Mexico.

The claimants were the Loewen Group, Inc. and Raymond L. Loewen, seeking damages under the Agreement. It was described as an "important and extremely difficult case." The respondent (defendant) was the United States of America. The tribunal castigated Judge Graves, the jury, and Jerry O'Keefe's lawyers in a scathing opinion covering over seventy pages. The following are paragraph quotes verbatim, taken directly from the decision:

Case No. ARB(CAF)/98/3.

53. Judge Graves failed in his duty to take control of the trial by permitting the jury to be exposed to persistent and flagrant appeals to prejudice on the part of O'Keefe's counsel and witnesses.

56. O'Keefe's strategy of presenting the case in this was linked to Jerry O'Keefe's fighting for his country against the Japanese and the exhortation in the closing address of Mr. Gary (lead counsel for O'Keefe) to the jury to do their duty as Americans and Mississippians.

61. The strategy of emphasizing O'Keefe's American nationality as against Loewen's Canadian origins reached a peak in Mr. Gary's closing address. He likened Jerry O'Keefe's struggle against Loewen with his wartime exploits against the Japanese, asserting that he was motivated by "pride in America" and "love for your country."

He described the American jury system as one that O'Keefe "Fought for and some died for" (Transcript at 5540-41).

119. By any standard of review, the tactics of O'Keefe's lawyers, particularly Mr. Gary, were impermissible. By any standard of evaluation, the trial judge failed to afford Loewen the process that was due.

215. Here we encounter the central difficulty in Loewen's case. Loewen failed to present evidence disclosing its reasons for entering into the settlement agreement in preference to pursuing other options,

223. Chapter Eleven of NAFTA represents a progressive development in international law whereby the individual investor may make a claim on its own behalf and submit the claim to international arbitration, as TLGI has done in the instant case.

242. ......The natural instinct, when someone observes a miscarriage of justice, is to step in and try to put it right, but the interests of the international investing community demand that we must observe the principles which we have been appointed to apply, and stay our hands.

The final order implementing the decision was signed by the three judges in Washington, D.C., on June 25, 2003. Of particular interest and peculiar as well, are the words contained in the last sentence of the Opinion, which seem to imply that the "interests of the international invested community" is paramount to the principles of the right to a jury trial contained in the United States Constitution.

Of particular derision and criticism was Gary's closing argument and the language contained therein, reflecting O'Keefe's service to his country, and the rights provided the foreign company as being equal to all parties who come before the court and the jury.

Notwithstanding, the caustic criticism by the international tribunal of our final argument, we were proud to be able to remind the jurors as to their duty to consider all litigants who appear before them as equals under our system of justice.

Loewen almost got away with it again, pleading for the American taxpayers to pay for his misdeeds and blaming the American judicial system for his problems. Like most giants of his ilk, they always blame someone else for their misdeeds and when they get caught with their hands in the cookie jar, they start making up their own rules. If Loewen and other corporate executives would just follow the rules at the very beginning of a decision-making event, they wouldn't find themselves facing multi-million dollar lawsuits for the damages suffered by the citizens of this country for their misdeeds and there would be no basis for juries to award verdicts in such eye popping amounts. The Loewen case remains one of Gary's favorite subjects in the endless, inspirational speeches he makes in African American churches and meeting halls throughout the nation. He revels in telling the tale of a great-great-grandson of slaves, championing the cause of a great-grandson of slave owners. "Only in this great nation of ours; only in America," Gary says.

"I've told him my family never owned slaves," O'Keefe says. "My great-grandfather was a dirt-poor farmer. Willie, he gets kind of carried away sometimes."

VIII

AL-PRO vs. DISNEY
EISNER'S MOUSE GETS TRAPPED

Corporations - An ingenious device for obtaining
individual profit without individual responsibility.
Ambrose Bierce, Devil's Dictionary

The half a billion dollar verdict Willie E. Gary achieved in a small Mississippi courtroom was the first case to bring him national attention. It likely would have faded to distant memory had he not shortly thereafter been awarded a jury verdict against the Walt *Disney Company*. It is perhaps ironic that this case was referred to him by the one American lawyer more famous than Gary, the late, Johnnie Cochran. Unlike most referring attorneys, Johnnie Cochran was not a lawyer expected to remain in the background of any lawsuit.

Johnnie Cochran and Willie Gary both are African American. Both have achieved amazing success as lawyers, competing in a profession largely dominated by Caucasians; however, there are very few other similarities in their astounding success stories.

Cochran was born in 1937 in Shreveport, Louisiana. His father, Johnnie L. Cochran, Sr., graduated Valedictorian of his class at Central Colored High School in Shreveport and was able to provide a stable life for his family, which included his son, two daughters and his wife.

Unlike Gary, Cochran had attended school full time, first in Shreveport and later in Los Angeles, California. He was encouraged to excel in his classes by both parents who hoped he would become a doctor. His childhood idol was Thurgood Marshall, who had been lead attorney in the case of Brown vs. Board of Education of Topeka, Kansas, in which the United States Supreme Court struck down the concept of "separate but equal" education in American schools. Marshall went on to become the first African American to serve as an associate justice of that Court.

Cochran graduated from Loyola Marymount University School of Law in 1962, and was admitted to the California Bar Association in 1963. His first job was with the Los Angeles City Attorney's Office as a deputy city attorney in the criminal division, where he prosecuted persons accused of committing various minor crimes. He left that job after only two years to enter private law practice with an established black attorney who specialized in criminal defense work. There was no shortage of clients from the outset, but just a few months later while the senior attorney was out of the state, Cochran found himself thrust into a series of cases that would erupt from one of America's more tragic events – race riots in the Watts section of Los Angeles.

In his recent book, *A Lawyer's Life*, Cochran describes the scene at his office following the riots:

"Four thousand people. And every one of them needed an attorney. Our phones started ringing and long lines began forming outside our office. We had more clients than I ever imagined possible. People were coming early in the morning till after midnight..."

"The Watt's riots marked the beginning of the racial explosion that would shake America over the next few years. But for me professionally, business could not possibly have been better. At night I would come home with my pockets filled with cash. We were making as much as $8,000 a day. Obviously that wasn't all my money, but enough of it was..."

By the end of 1965, Cochran was ready to open his own office. He went on to accomplish a strong reputation throughout southern California as a premier criminal defense attorney with a large African American client base whose cases kept him frequently in the public eye. These efforts led to a number of successful civil lawsuits against the Los Angeles Police Department for its members' consistent brutality against African Americans. This brutality finally led to the United States government, placing the department under federal supervision.

One thing lead to another. His success against the police attracted many famous black entertainers to his office, either for defense in criminal cases or assistance in civil disputes. He became active in many African American organizations. It was hardly a surprise when he finally received a telephone call from the Los Angeles County Jail. Famed NFL player, O.J. Simpson, was unhappy with his lawyers.

At first, Cochran refused to enter the case. The defense team was headed by Robert Shapiro, who earlier had received national attention defending Senator Edward Kennedy's nephew in a Florida rape case. Cochran had worked as an expert commentator on the case with Tom Brokaw on the *NBC Nightly News* during the preliminary hearing. In *A Lawyer's Life*, Cochran states that he was surprised by the defense team's actions in the Simpson case, forming the opinion that Simpson's lawyers had not formed "a cohesive strategy." Cochran stated, "It rather seemed like they were responding to each crises as it occurred."

Simpson's calls kept coming. Finally, Cochran agreed to join the team and in a few short weeks, Shapiro was gone. Cochran was in charge. The rest is history.

Fresh from his stunning victory in the O.J. Simpson criminal trial, Cochran was besieged with calls and letters from people throughout the nation seeking his representation. Millions of people had remained glued to their television sets watching Cochran and Simpson's "Dream Team" of attorneys dismantle the prosecution's claim that the famed athlete and movie star had brutally assassinated his former wife, Nicole Brown, and her boyfriend, Ron Goldman, in the driveway of her California home.

Following that victory, Cochran was interviewed on numerous network television shows and was the regular subject of jokes, both cruel and complimentary, in every form of American entertainment. He had been the brunt of David Letterman's humor, made personal appearances on *Saturday Night Live* and *The Roseanne Show*, as well as being the subject of several one-line wise cracks in various popular movies. His fame became such that he moved much of his operation to New York City and his offices, known as The Cochran

Firm, had 120 lawyers in eight different states.

It is no wonder that a former baseball umpire, Nick Stracik, and architect Ed Russell, wrote to Cochran seeking his help in a lawsuit then pending against the Disney Company, the entertainment giant that had grown on the shoulders of Mickey Mouse. That letter had somehow caught the attention of Cochran's longtime associate and co-counsel in the Simpson trial, Carl Douglas. He discusses the case in the closing pages of *A Lawyer's Life* by stating:

"I met with Stracik and Russell and they had an abundance of evidence. Without question, they had been involved in a development arrangement with Disney. Disney had ended that relationship and proceeded without them. I was confident we could prove that. However, I was less confident we could get a jury in Orlando - where the case would have to be tried - to make Disney pay for it. A large decision against that company could hurt their community."

The Walt *Disney Company* is known throughout the world as a source of seemingly endless entertainment for people of all ages, races and religions. It enjoys an annual, gross income in excess of $26 billion for entertaining and informing people around the globe. Many financial experts consider it one of the world's most lucrative business empires.

It all started with a mouse. In March 1928, Walter Elias Disney was a twenty-six-year-old cartoonist taking a tedious, five-day train trip from New York to Los Angeles. He marked time with his sketchpad, devising a variation on his existing cartoon character,

Oswald the Lucky Rabbit. The ears were shortened. The feet got shoes. Mickey Mouse was born. Disney and his brother, Roy, already had produced over sixty cartoon features for Hollywood about a character named, "Alice." They had begun producing "Oswald" features, but were faced with severe economic problems and were embroiled in a number of business disputes that would see them lose the rights to both characters to former associates and employees.

Having been victimized by the greed of others and losing the benefits of more than five years of his creative efforts, the young artist took steps to prevent a reoccurrence of such a disaster. On May 21, 1928, the United States Patent Office received Disney's trademark application for the use of Mickey Mouse in films. The application was granted on August 2, 1929, and later would be the basis for his victory in a lawsuit against a competitor for attempting to steal the lovable, little character.

In 1955, Disney launched Disneyland in California as a fabulous, $17 million Magic Kingdom that would attract more than 250 million visitors over the next thirty years. His success in California directed his attention to the east, where he wanted to open yet another theme park. His uncanny sense for consumer preferences prompted him to focus on Florida.

In 1964 and 1965, Disney executives began traveling to Orange County in central Florida to acquire land. They registered under false names. Disney remained in California, fearing that he would be recognized and rumors of his interest would cause land prices to spiral. As large parcels of property started changing hands, rumors indeed did fester. Finally, as the purchases neared completion, media attention became too intense for the secret to continue. Disney formally announced his intentions shortly before the acquisition process was completed. Land prices escalated from $183 per acre to more than a thousand dollars. In all, he would acquire 43 square miles of virgin land, twice the size of New York's Manhattan Island.

Walter Elias Disney died on December 15, 1966, just two weeks after his sixty-fifth birthday. Walt Disney World opened its doors nearly five years later, on October 1, 1971. Eleven years later Epcot Center was opened to the public. Today, with the addition of two Universal Studios theme parks, Orange County, Florida prospers as one of the world's most popular vacation spots. Its residents depend heavily on the Disney empire for their economic well-being. The political infrastructure, its judiciary included, surely knows where its bread and butter come from.

These facts were not lost on Johnnie Cochran. In *A Lawyer's Life*, he refers to this economic dependence as the major drawback to accepting the Stracik and Russell case. In fact, he indicates that he was unsure whether victory over Mickey Mouse in Orlando, Florida, was even possible. He reported that he believed Willie Gary was the best lawyer in the country for the matter, and that he persuaded "The Giant Killer" to work on the matter with him so, at least, they could send the Disney company a loud message.

Personally, I don't know anything about Gary agreeing to take the case because he wanted to send Disney a message; however, I do know that he wanted me to find out if the case could be won and if so, whether I thought it would be worth all the time and money needed to handle it. Cases like that cost hundreds of thousands of dollars, even millions to pursue. I reviewed the initial materials provided to me and told Gary we must meet with Cochran immediately. He agreed. Cochran sent an associate of his and we all met in Orlando. With us, was Mel Silverman, an intellectual property lawyer who had commenced the case in the federal court in Orlando, Florida. Upon their arrival, we learned the pending lawsuit was on the verge of dismissal in federal court. That case essentially asserted that Disney had violated federal copyright laws in stealing the idea for a sports complex that the client had presented to Disney as an adjunct to the highly successful Orlando theme park.

The federal judge disagreed with that legal theory and dismissed the lawsuit; however, the judge did allow a thirty-day grace period to file a new case in state court. It was within this thirty-day window that we entered the case.

We felt the decision of the federal court to dismiss the case was a blessing in disguise. We disdain the federal court system. The judges are generally very conservative, appointed for life as a political gift, usually not in touch with the common man and not favorable to plaintiff's lawyers. They severely restrict lawyers in the pre-trial questioning of prospective jurors; therefore, we were pleased that a state judge and jury would hear our case, which meant that the rules would be favorable to our manner of trying the lawsuit.

One of the principals of the client company, Nick Stracik was extremely upset and unhappy by the dismissal of the case by the federal judge. He blamed the lawyers for the dismissal in the most strident language, laced with obscenities. I had heard similar outbursts and use of such language years before by drill sergeants in World War II. Stracik's behavior became routine, as we would hear these outbursts with every set back we encountered during the case.

It was a strong case, as far as the law was concerned, and we had excellent facts to support the claim. The initial problem was whether the case could survive the defense assaults based on some vague, legal technicalities. If it could, the major problem clearly was the location where the trial would take place. It would have to be tried in Orlando. Disney owns Orlando - lock, stock and barrel. Once we got past the legal hurdles, I was worried about the composition of the jury we would draw. We were also concerned about Stracik's credibility, and how the jury would react to his testimony, especially under cross-examination. Frankly, had it not been for some fairly typical defense attorney blunders, and some utterly unbelievable testimony by the Disney people, we could well have lost the case. We had agreed our theory of the case would not rest under a violation of a copyright law, but under a Florida statute governing trade secrets. Our case was on the claim that Disney had committed a theft of our "trade secret." Whether it was a "trade secret" and if so, whether or not it had been "stolen" were technical legal issues that a judge and jury would have to determine.

No sooner had we filed the case in the Orange County Courthouse and had Disney served with the new complaint, that we were greeted with a motion to dismiss the case. The motion was on the basis that the federal court's prior dismissal of the case effectively precluded our case from proceeding in the state court. It was a fairly routine and expected motion and we felt confident that it would be summarily rejected by the court. I argued against the motion being granted before the new judge, leaving the courthouse confident that the judge would rule in our favor. To our shock, an order was received within a week, granting Disney's motion to dismiss the case with prejudice, which meant that our case was over, we could not proceed and we were out of court. Most dismissals of cases at this stage of litigation are, without prejudice, meaning that we could amend the complaint to allege other facts to support our case and we could remain in court. Such was not the case here, however, and it was a serious legal setback.

On hearing of this dismissal, Stracik went into his anger management uncontrollable mode again and not without some justification. He insisted on calling in the press, *60 Minutes* TV program, and others, to claim that there was a conspiracy between Disney and the judge and he wanted that "conspiracy" aspect explored and exposed. I was not a happy lawyer at that time as well. After all, I had drafted the complaint, confident it would survive any Disney attack, and here I was, not even in the batter's box yet and the game is over. I reacted to the group assembled to discuss our new course of action. I promised them that if we lost the case on the appeal of the dismissal, I would recognize it as the time for me to "hang up my shingle" which I offered to do. Only Stracik agreed in his usual colorful vocabulary, stating that I should follow my suggestion as that would be a smart thing for me to do.

We immediately hired appellate counsel and commenced the necessary procedures to file the appeal to overturn the dismissal of the case and return the case to the lower court for trial. Oral arguments were made before the three-judge panel and on Feb. 26, 1999, the Fifth District Court of Appeal for the state of Florida rendered its decision stating in part, that the federal court, in dismissing the copyright claims, did not preclude us from proceeding in the state court on a different legal theory. Stracik was pleased when we notified him and told me I could "stick around" for the rest of the trial. There were times thereafter that I regretted that I had.

I was seventy-two years old and, once again, found myself at the forefront of a massive effort against a giant company in its own backyard. Gary was busy trying other cases, enhancing his charitable efforts and launching his new television network. Cochran was commuting from California to New York, where he was hosting a series of television talk shows for *Court TV*, while defending rap star and entrepreneur, Sean "Puffy" Combs, in a criminal case and developing a huge national law firm.

The case was returned to the lower court and we picked up where we had left off, accumulating additional facts to support our claim. With everything I found, though, I could not anticipate the blunders that the Disney people would make once the trial began. I don't know quite how to put it, but over the years, I have concluded that Gary's presence has some kind of numbing effect on the opposition. It is as though the defense lawyers try to beat Gary at his own game, as if they want to do what Gary does with jurors. That just does not happen. Nobody does what Willie Gary does, better than Willie Gary himself.

I found a plethora of facts to work with. In all I uncovered 108 similarities between Disney's Wide World of Sports and the sports

The Giant Killers

complex planned, designed and submitted by Stracik and Russell to Disney, years before. They ranged from the overall concept down to the identical number of parking spaces and the same number of seats. Wide World of Sports also had the same number and types of different venues proposed by the two men. It had the same center for Latin American sports studies initially suggested by them, as well as a television sports broadcasting school, a referee and umpire school, and an invitation to house the American Amateur Union, the world's largest amateur sporting organization, all of which had been included in the proposal first provided by Stracik and Russell.

In order to prove a claim that "trade secrets" had been stolen, we had to show that the subject matter was unique. In this case, it had to be shown that the concept of such a sports complex submitted to Disney was different from anything else generally known or developed. Disney lawyers claimed the idea was fairly common, that similar ideas and entities existed elsewhere. The team of lawyers we had assembled located experts to repudiate that claim. These included a sports marketing expert from the Georgia Dome, and a representative from the Nike five-star basketball camp. Both would testify that they had traveled throughout the world and never encountered anything similar to the Wide World of Sports concept conceived by our clients.

Our team also secured an architecture professor who would attest to the similarities between the plans submitted by our clients to Disney's Wide World of Sports. An economist formerly employed by the United States Securities and Exchange Commission would testify that the Disney sports venue was worth between $200 million and $500 million.

As the case developed, concern grew that a jury from conservative, Orange County, Florida, might not be receptive to Johnnie Cochran. He was fresh from international attention gained from the O.J. Simpson trial; a case that many believe further polarized the African American and white communities. Some of the people working with me assembling the case feared that many potential jurors might be offended by Cochran's involvement, reasoning they likely would be among the white conservatives of our society who felt that a black man succeeded in getting away with the brutal murder of a white woman. As it turned out, it was the Disney lawyers who handled the Cochran problem for us.

Johnnie Cochran was not there the first day of trial. He had some other matter out of the state and did not get in until the second or third day. Apparently, the defense team had concerns about his fame as well. One of their lawyers asked the entire jury panel if any of them had any preconceived opinions about Cochran and eleven out of twenty-five raised their hands. When he pressed the point, they all said they found him offensive from what they had seen on television in the Simpson case. The judge excused all eleven of them.

Earlier, Gary had approached the sensitive subject of Cochran's controversial role as O.J. Simpson's lead lawyer. The jurors response had been cool, but not such that it would necessarily justify excluding anyone from hearing the case. The defense posed the question to the prospective jurors in a way that would leave little doubt that certain jurors most likely would punish us for having

Cochran on our trial team. The trial transcript reads:

"Now, could I please see a show of hands of anybody in this courtroom who simply, because Johnnie Cochran is one of the lawyers for the plaintiffs, cannot look at the evidence, hear the testimony, and give a fair and impartial verdict? Please raise your hands and let me know who you are."

This was one of Disney's lead lawyers asking the question. Gary had some of the jurors admit they were less than thrilled with Johnnie Cochran. But the defense spelled it right out. "Look at the evidence?" "Hear the testimony?" "Give a fair and impartial verdict?" It is the very definition of a juror's duty. The judge had no choice. He excused every one of them from serving on our jury.

When Cochran did show up, all the remaining jurors were smiling and beaming at him as though he was some kind of celebrity. Well, actually, he was. From that point forward, he just charmed them to death. It was as if they had demonstrated some sort of loyalty to him and he wanted them to know how much he appreciated that. I think many of them had their minds made up early on that they were going to give Johnnie Cochran something, maybe to make up for the way the others had said they felt about him.

Willie Gary and Johnnie Cochran were in the same courtroom, trying the same case. Both were black. Both were famous. Six jurors – one black and five white, would now judge the Walt *Disney Company*, the gargantuan media and entertainment giant that has entertained millions throughout the world and had put Orlando on the map. They had been yanked from their passive lives for five weeks to decide right from wrong and to put a dollar value on their decision, while the whole world watched.

Trial would last twenty-five days, before the three men and three women on the jury would return a verdict that once again would shine a national spotlight on Willie Gary and send corporate America sputtering to the media about a runaway jury system.

The media was crawling all over the place. Cameras were rolling, flashbulbs were popping and reporters were lurking around every corner with tape recorders raised in people's faces, pen and paper in hand. It was the stuff movies are made about, but I doubt the Disney folks would produce it.

We were seeking $1.4 billion for our clients, a retired minor league baseball umpire and an architect. The $1.4 billion purportedly represented all of Disney's profits on everything from Mickey Mouse watches to Cinderella movie rights in 1999. The amount claimed seemed fair and provided Gary with some basis for the elusive billion dollar verdict he sought.

The company spent $103 million to build the complex. The year before trial more than a million people visited the facility, mostly students and amateur athletes competing in sporting events and tournaments ranging from baseball to gymnastics. Disney consistently claimed it lost money on the complex, rather than showing a profit.

Gary and Cochran divided up the principal trial duties. From the outset, as in every case before or since, Gary relied upon his down-home approach to the jury. Before questioning prospective jurors, Judge Coleman allowed the attorneys an opportunity to explain their case to the panel of people assembled for selection. As usual, Gary skillfully turned this process into an opening argument designed to sway jurors before the first word of testimony was heard. He started by identifying himself as just a friendly guy from humble beginnings. The trial transcript reads:

MR. GARY: "Good afternoon members of the prospective jury. As the judge has indicated, my name is Willie Gary. As a matter of fact, I practice law down in South Florida. I'm from a little farming town called Indiantown. Anybody ever heard of Indiantown, Florida? Let me see your hands if you've heard of it. I knew I was from a famous city."

As he proceeded, Gary associated himself and his cause with a religious exercise, an approach he uses in every trial where the opportunity presents itself, explaining in a subtle way, how his clients' claim really arose from a breach of the Lord's law.

MR. GARY: "How many of you are wondering what this case is really about? Let me see a show of hands if you're wondering what this case is about. Okay? Thank you. Now, let me ask this question - how many of you have heard of one of those commandments, and there's ten of them that are called the Ten Commandments, 'thou shalt not steal?' Have you ever heard of that commandment? Let me see a show of hands of those who heard of that commandment. Have you heard of that? Let me see your hands. Well, members of the jury, the evidence in this case is going to show that this case is about fraud; it's about stealing, conspiracy, cover-up, deceit and, above all, it's about the greatest sin that's known to man, and that's greed, the all-mighty dollar."

The biblical reference continued smoothly to an unspoken David versus Goliath scenario.

MR. GARY: "It's about taking advantage of the little guy because they knew they could get away with it because of their power, their size, and their influence. Members of the jury, the evidence will show in this case that these men, specifically in this case, worked years to put hundreds of thousands of dollars in developing a concept, you might want to call it a dream, to do the All-Pro Sports Complex, which is now known as the Disney's Wide World of Sports. Members of the jury, the evidence will show, based on the documents and the evidence, that Disney stole, stole their dream."

Gary also managed to inject his theme of patriotism as adroitly as he has in numerous other cases.

MR. GARY: "They stole from these people. And Disney, that's why we're here. And I don't care how big you are or how powerful you are, in America you can't trample on anybody just because of their size. I don't care how much money you have, you can't do it."

Without missing a beat, Gary used his reference to the defendant's supposed wealth to set up prospective jurors for a large award, carefully studying the reaction from each of them as he did so.

MR. GARY: "The experts will tell you that the damages in this case could exceed a billion dollars, and you're going to hear from these experts. You're going to hear from the economists; you're going to hear from the architects. Oh yes, they will tell you that the damages for what was stolen, the unjust enrichment by Disney, could exceed a billion dollars."

Now, in less than twenty minutes Gary has told jurors that the Disney Company has violated God's law and the American way of life. He has emphasized it as a rich and powerful company and that our clients are poor, helpless men left to the mercy of this giant because they trusted Mickey Mouse. I have seen many lawyers try to pull off that sort of thing. I have seen few who succeeded in the effort. Gary does it out of hand.

Throughout the trial, Gary and Cochran plowed through Disney executives like farmers cutting wheat. Like so many businessmen, they responded to questions by trying to avoid them with vague and misleading answers. They were playing right into the skilled litigators' hands.

It never is possible to say that any one event, any one shred of evidence or any one, particular exhibit carries the day in a trial. Standing alone, it is highly unlikely that actually happens in any case. In the Disney trial, however, testimony from an economist surely had an impact on the jurors. As so often occurs in Gary's cases, the testimony resulted from an over reaching defense attorney trying to press a point too far.

While hard-pressed to claim the Disney Company was broke or destitute, the company lawyers continuously hammered that the Wide World of Sports Complex was a losing investment. Our economist disagreed with the assertion and was undergoing rigorous cross-examination about the basis for all his opinions. The attorney carried his attack too far when asking for all the criteria used by the economist in establishing the company's annual income the previous year. His response was simple. The wages paid to Chief Executive Officer Michael Eisner, which had amounted to $600 million.

We knew he had been paid that much. We spent hours trying to figure out a way to get that before the jurors. The rules of evidence simply would not allow us to do it. If we had tried, it could have caused a mistrial and we would have had to start all over again. But here he was, hammering away at our expert and getting carried away with the sound of his own voice. I sensed it was coming. Our expert knew we wanted it in evidence. He knew we could not get it in. Then bang, there it was. A half dozen heads snapped up in the jury box. These jurors were simple folks. They got up and went to work every day struggling to make enough money to make ends meet. One of them cleaned other people's houses for a living. What could she earn in a year? Maybe $25,000? If you do the math, I think it would have taken her something like 4,000 years to make as much money as Eisner made the year before.

During the course of the trial, we went to Los Angeles and took the deposition of Michael Eisner, the Disney chairman and CEO. He swore that he had never heard of All-Pro Sports Camps, nor had any Disney executives told him about All-Pro's plans or about meetings with Stracik and Russell; however, Ed Russell testified that he met with Disney's head architect in 1997 and gave Disney attorneys All-Pro's plans for a sports complex.

As the case progressed, we became increasingly confident that we would succeed in obtaining a verdict in our favor. Although there were settlement discussions conducted off and on during the course of the trial, we were too far apart to believe that any settlement could be achieved until the case had been concluded. Therefore, we prepared to proceed and planed the final argument to be presented to the jury.

We worked together on the instructions that we would present to the judge to be read to the jury, as to the law that the jury must follow in reaching a verdict. We believed that the instructions we submitted to the court were very favorable, and we were pleased when he agreed to most of those that we had submitted. We also prepared and submitted the verdict form that the jury would complete after they had finished their deliberations. The jury retired to consider and deliberate on the case. As in every case, that is the most trying time for the lawyers, because all of the work and the effort now rest in the hands of the six jurors.

We returned to the hotel and waited several hours until we received a call from the court that the jury had arrived at its verdict and that we were to return to the courtroom immediately.

We settled ourselves down at the lawyer's tables and stood when the jury entered the courtroom, in their somber way, looking at no one. The judge asked if they had arrived at a verdict and the foreman announced they had and handed the verdict form to the clerk, who delivered it to the judge. The judge reviewed it and handed it back to the clerk to read.

Although we were confident, there is always tremendous tension and apprehension by everyone in the courtroom at that time. The first question was, "Did any defendant misappropriate one or more of the trade secrets belonging to the plaintiffs?" When the answer was "yes," our elation was difficult to conceal without displaying any emotion. As each question was answered by the jury in our favor, we waited for the final question to be asked, as to the amount of damages to be awarded to plaintiff. The answer came: "Two Hundred and Forty Million Dollars." We were barely able to constrain ourselves, but as soon as the judge granted a recess, the courtroom erupted in pandemonium. After the verdict was rendered, the jurors asked if they could have their picture taken with us in the courtroom. Of course, we were happy to oblige. The jurors were jostling a bit to get as close to Cochran as they could.

The newspapers reported that Disney's general counsel appeared stunned by the verdict. The *Orlando Sentinel*, on August 20, 2000, reported that Disney filed for a retrial alleging that the attorneys for businessmen Nicholas Stracik and Edward Russell improperly swayed jurors through a "populous rhetoric and anti-business prejudice" by casting Disney as a big corporation trampling on the little guys. This, of course, was true. The newspaper article continues: "Disney says jurors were barred from hearing key evidence and that jurors were prejudiced by the improper tactics of All Pro attorney, Willie Gary, one of the nations top trial attorneys." The article continued: "Bob Parenti, Gary's law partner in Stuart, dismissed Disney's claims. 'This judgment is firm, it's solid, it's well tried, and there isn't an error in it.' Parenti said, 'There is not going to be any basis for a new trial.'"

Disney filed a Notice of Appeal, to appeal the verdict and posted a bond to secure the judgment. Settlement negotiations, as is usual in a case of this type, were entered into immediately and after various meetings, the case was settled under conditions of confidentiality. Although the settlement figure was never publicly disclosed, we celebrated, as usual, with the legal team and staff through the evening with copious amounts of "Dom" to quench our thirst. We autographed a photograph of the lawyers and passed it out to the group gathered, as a memento of that historic legal victory.

Gary had to look to the next case involving another "Giant," Anheuser- Busch, to renew his quest for that elusive billion-dollar verdict.

MARIS vs. ANHEUSER-BUSCH
BORN-ON DATE MISCARRIES

You never expected justice from a company, did you?
They have neither a soul to lose, nor a body to kick.
LORD THURLOW, 1 Holland, Memoir of Sydney Smith 331

On October 1, 1961, Roger Maris lofted a home run into the right field porch at Yankee Stadium, ending the thirty-year record for major league home runs set by Babe Ruth in 1927. Many die-hard fans refused to accept the feat as beating the legendary Babe's record. Ruth stroked his sixty homers in 154 games. Maris required 161 games, the record breaker occurring only in the last game of the season. Baseball Commissioner Ford Frick, once a friend of Ruth's, insisted that the accomplishment be noted with an asterisk in the record books.

Forty years later, the Roger Maris name would be linked with Willie Gary's when a Gainesville, Florida jury would award Maris Distributing Company a verdict against the "King of Beers," Anheuser-Busch. Willie E. Gary would add another gold tag to his record of victories.

Maris was the son of first-generation Croatian Americans. He emerged into the world of baseball from the American Legion

League in Fargo, North Dakota, where he was raised. The Roger Maris Museum and the MeritCare Roger Maris Cancer Center now are located in Fargo and his remains are entered at the city's Holy Cross Cemetery.

Maris was a stubborn man. When he first signed with the Cleveland Indians, the rookie insisted that he be allowed to serve his minor league apprenticeship with his hometown's Fargo Moorhead Twins. When told it was against team policy to allow a rookie to play ball in his hometown because it subjected him to too much pressure, Maris is said to have replied, "Not me. I'm going to Fargo. That's definite. Now it's up to you to decide whether I go there just to live on my own or whether I go there to play ball for Cleveland." He went to Fargo.

Maris retired from baseball a bitter man in 1968, the same year I took office as president of my local bar association.

I was not much of a baseball fan. I remember reading about the Babe's record being broken and I recall stories about the race between Roger Maris and Mickey Mantle to break the record.

Mickey Mantle clearly was baseball's favorite Yankee in 1961. Most of that year he and Maris were neck and neck in the race to break Ruth's record. It was Mantle, however, who thrilled fans with dramatic, 500-foot home runs and who garnered fan support to break the legend's record.

Maris played four more seasons with the Yankees, before being traded to the St. Louis Cardinals, where he lasted two more years and was considered quite useful to that team's two successive National League pennants.

While Maris may not have received anything of great value for his sixty-one home runs, his two years with St. Louis had earned him the gratitude of team owner, August Busch III. The beer baron rewarded him with an Anheuser-Busch beer distributorship in Gainesville, Florida. Few people realize how profitable a beer distributorship can be, particularly if it gives one the exclusive right to distribute Budweiser in the home of the University of Florida, Gators. Drinking beer is a favorite pastime of football fans as it is in every college town.

Selling the "King of Beers" earned Maris and his family millions upon millions of dollars, a largess that continued for his extended family well over a decade after Maris died of lymphatic cancer in 1985 at the young age of fifty-one. Gussie Busch's generous gift continued handsomely to provide for the Maris family until the mid 1990s, when the Anheuser-Busch Company decided to terminate the relationship.

The agreement between Anheuser-Busch and Roger Maris provided it could only be terminated by mutual consent, or if the distributor somehow was guilty of fraud. The company claimed to pride itself on selling "fresh" beer, marking its labels with the date it was brewed called the "born on date." It was required that the beer be sold within 110 days of that date, otherwise, as Busch claimed, the beer would become "skunky" or unpalatable to the taste of serious beer drinkers. It was our position that their claim was nothing more than a marketing ploy and beer drinkers could not care less on the date when beer was born. If a drinker was seriously interested, he could never locate the date on the can or bottle anyway nor read it if once found. Then one would have to add the 110 days to determine if it was out of date or not.

We maintained during the trial that it was just another scheme dreamed up by Busch to justify termination of dealerships if they, through their seditious forages through marketing outlets, found "out of date" beer.

During the trial, Busch brought its chief brew master, a portly gentleman who spoke with a heavy German accent, in to testify. He stated without equivocation that "fresh" beer is the most important desire of a beer drinker; however, on cross- examination, he conceded that beer shipped to Europe on ocean freighters frequently did not arrive until after the expiration of the "born on date" and that deficiency never seemed to bother German drinkers. We knew then, by the jurors practically laughing aloud in reaction to that testimony, that the jury would never accept the claim by Busch regarding the sale of "stale" beer. It was nothing more than a specious ploy, as were their other claims, in an attempt to avoid responsibilities under the terms of their contract.

Other items cited by Busch included: metal supporting beams that were painted red instead of white, trucks parked in the grass at the warehouse site, and failure to employ more workers. They also claimed the distributorship was too profitable, and the delivery trucks were old and should be replaced. In response to that, Rudy Maris, Roger's older brother and head of the business, stated that such claims were frivolous, did not justify termination, and that it was an intimidation scheme to drive the Maris family out of business and acquire the profitable distributorship for themselves.

To enforce their self-proclaimed standards, the company maintains regional Market Evaluation Teams (MET), that periodically pay unannounced visits to retailers where the beer is sold to check the sell-by dates on the bottles. Anheuser-Busch claimed that the Maris family's inventory of beer was kept in old coolers that failed to maintain the proper temperature and that the beer was left for sale beyond the sales cut off dates. These claims were never proven.

The company also alleged that the sale of old, warm beer, a violation of Anheuser-Busch policy, constituted a fraud on the company and, further, since the company assured the beer drinking public that its beer was fresh, such sales also were a fraud to the public.

Anticipating the termination, Maris sought out the help of an experienced attorney, Bernie Dempsey, in Orlando, Florida. Dempsey had been a former federal prosecutor in the middle district in Florida and known to be an aggressive litigator. He entered private practice in the '70s. In 1982, he hired a young lawyer, Manuel "Manny" Socias, who worked with him until 1990 at which time Socias left to begin his own practice. When Maris contacted Dempsey, the first lawyer to assist him was Socias, who later became a principal litigator in the Maris trial.

Dempsey decided to pre-empt Busch's anticipated termination, and commenced a lawsuit in the federal court requesting an injunction to prevent Busch from terminating the contract with Maris, claiming that a provision of the distributorship agreement preventing public companies from owning a beer distributorship was anti-competitive and violated anti-trust and monopoly laws.

Busch had hired an internationally known firm from Washington, D.C., that had represented Busch in previous termination cases. Peter Moll was the chief and principal trial litigator and had never lost a case while representing Busch. His record remained intact as, after a six-week trial, Busch had won another federal case, which was dismissed.

Wisely, Dempsey and Socias, on behalf of Maris, had also filed a lawsuit in state court alleging claims under state law including defamation, wrongful contract termination and interference with Maris' business relations. That case was pending when we entered the case.

From the time the lawsuit was filed on January 3, 1997, by our predecessors, until the trial started on May 1, 2001, more that 125 witnesses were deposed. Many of these depositions lasted several days. Maris family members alone faced sixty-two days in depositions as defense lawyers tried to create conflicts in their testimony for later use in trial. There were seventy-four hearings before four successive judges assigned to the case by the time we entered the case.

It is not uncommon that we enter cases of this magnitude after they have been commenced by other courtroom lawyers who realize, while in battle, that it cannot be won without the assistance of contingency fee lawyers who are willing to take the risk of a loss, for the opportunity of a just reward. The client realizes that too, as did Rudy Maris after expending over $20 million dollars on attorney fees and expenses without a favorable jury verdict in hand.

I was part of the initial team with Madison McClellan, a

young trial lawyer who was now a partner in our firm. Madison was very effective in the Disney trial and had the skills and personality that we felt necessary before a Gainesville jury. He was a graduate of the University of Florida and well known in the Gainesville area where the trial was to be held.

We traveled with a group of lawyers and paralegals to Ocala to visit the Maris warehouse and we were greeted by members of the Maris family who escorted us through their offices. The walls displayed numerous photographs of Roger Maris and his trophies, all proudly displayed and rightly so. We entered a cavernous warehouse the size of which seemed to equal a football field.

Covering the entire floor were packing boxes and files comprising the depositions, court transcripts and exhibits that had been utilized up to this point and the trial had not even yet started. We wondered individually and collectively whether we could be prepared to assimilate all of this and be adequately prepared to battle one of the most tenacious legal adversaries I had ever witnessed or encountered in my career.

We would soon find out that Busch's lawyers were not the typical silk-stocking defense firms who usually play within the common bounds of legal courtesy, but a team who attempted to take advantage of every legal trial artifice recorded. In essence, the trial eroded into a battle between lawyers and their trial conduct, and the merits of the claims between the parties were relegated to a secondary role of importance. It also demonstrated how corporate giants attempt to manipulate, control and dictate professional conduct of their lawyers as well as their attempt to subvert the proper function of the judicial system.

Willie Gary fired the first salvo of the war. Shortly after entering the case, he called a press conference in Gainesville held on the courthouse steps. He assembled a sizable contingency standing along side him behind the podium as he was introduced. The conference was recorded:

Maris Press Conference
MARCH 14, 2001
[All parties walking to podium.]

VOICE: "Ladies and Gentlemen, Willie E. Gary from Stuart, Florida."

WILLIE GARY: "Well, first of all, let me express thanks to all of you for being here, uh, today, uh. This is a proud day for the Maris family. I know Roger would be smiling if he could see us, and I know he can, because we are here to carry on something that he fought for so hard, to build and uh, that was the Maris Distributing business.

"As you all know, we are in litigation. This case has been going on now for some five years. And, I thank Roger, Jr. and above all, Rudy Maris, for thinking enough of our law firm to get us involved in this case. To bring us into the case.

"And, uh, when I think about the commitment that Anheuser-

Busch made to Roger, and Rudy, back in the late "60s when they took on this distributorship, because, at that time you had uh, August Busch, who was alive then, a man that I just feel, that if he knew what was going on today, no doubt he'd roll over in his grave. But it probably wouldn't surprise him that August Busch III is trying to drive this family out of business. Because August Busch III drove his own father out of business. And this family worked hard to build this business. They worked by the sweat of their brow. Put in a lot of early days and late nights. They took nothing and made something out of it. This distributorship became the number one distributorship, we think, in this country, for Anheuser-Busch. And then, greed set in – corporate greed. There is no doubt in my mind that we are here fighting this lawsuit today because of corporate greed. They're big; they're rich; they're powerful. And they feel, like with some other companies, that they can take what they want, when they want it. And how they want it.

"This business was the number one distributorship business in the country. And August Busch III set out to take it from this family. And that's what they tried to do. And they have done it for the most part. But we don't come seeking charity. We don't come with a lawsuit that's about something for nothing. This is about justice. It's about justice for a family that played by the rules; played by the rules and worked their fingers to the bone to build this business. We feel that the damages in this case, by the time this trial is over, will exceed $2.5 billion. $2.5

billion. No charity. Only justice. So, we're saying to corporate America, and particularly Anheuser-Busch, no more. We know you have twenty-seven lawyers on the other side. We know you have the money and you have the power. But at some point you're going to have to realize that we're going to fight for what we believe is right. And that's all we're doing. That's all this family is doing. Fighting for what they built; fighting for what is theirs; nothing more; nothing less.

"And I have the opportunity to introduce two of my clients this morning, who will make a brief statement. And I am so proud of meeting them. And let me just say this – those of you that know my law firm, we take on many cases around the country, but never before have I been any more proud to represent a client or a family than this family. They are truly, truly an all-American family. Believing only in what's right, and what's fair. And at this time I'm going to have Roger Maris, Jr. come to you; the son of the legend, Roger Maris, to speak to you. Let's give him a hand as he comes up."

[Applause.]

ROGER MARIS, JR.: "Thank you, Willie. This lawsuit is something that we wanted to avoid at all costs. But due to the way our family has been treated, we felt we were left with no other option. My father was the hardest working man I ever knew. On the field, off the field, and in the board room.

It is our duty to defend his good name, which branded our highly successful company, for years and years, until it was wrongfully taken away. This case isn't about dollars and cents; this case is about what is right and what is wrong. And God willing, we will make right the wrong that has been done to our family. Thank you for coming."

[Applause.]

WILLIE GARY: "Thank you Roger. And at this time, we are going to have a statement from Rogers's brother, the man that brought me here, to be a part of this case, Rudy Maris. Let's give him a hand."

[Applause.]

RUDY MARIS: "Thank you. My brother Roger and I started our distributorship in 1968. And we worked hard to make it one of the most profitable in the state of Florida, and one of the most successful beer distributorships in the country. What you see behind me is three generations of the Marises who have worked countless hours over the past thirty years to make Maris Distributing Company the best. We've built this company; we want it back; we want this injustice to be reversed. I thank you."

REPORTER: "Why allow – why allow Bernie Little to take

over that Ocala Distributorship, versus the Maris family, I mean, what's the advantage to Anheuser-Busch?"

WILLIE GARY: "Because Bernie is August Busch III's next-door neighbor, and they are friends. And down the road I can assure you that some hanky panky will take place. You see, that's what this whole thing is about. Not only just favoritism and a buddy system, but a business relationship that we feel will allow August Busch III and somebody within that family to end up with the business. August Busch couldn't do it directly, so he went through the back door with his friends. That's really what we're talking about here. Any other questions? If not, again – oh you have a question?"

REPORTER: "I just wanted to ask you for a business card."

Willie was eager to oblige. I was not present at that conference but the mission was accomplished. I am of the old school, literally and figuratively as one who has learned from experience, that the less said to the press during litigation the better, as those events may come back to haunt you later and so it happened here.

Prospective jurors questioned before jury service frequently express disdain for trial lawyers and would rather have their sons or daughters be CEOs of major corporations rather than lawyers appearing in the courtroom seeking damages for negligence resulting in injury to an innocent party. Corporate CEOs are universally considered as a standard for integrity, honesty and fair dealing, until fairly recent times when the trial bar began to unravel corporate business tactics and we began to see a modicum of executives in jail. More will probably follow since the crash of 2008.

So it is, that the press conference is now considered an appropriate counter attack to present the clients case to the public that generally has been pre-conditioned to be anti-plaintiff, anti-lawyer and pro-business. The only legal restraint, ethically, is that the conference should not be used to have a detrimental effect on the trial, otherwise, its fair game. Notwithstanding that standard, Busch's lawyers wasted no time to rush to the court, with a complaint alleging that Willie E. Gary and Madison McClellan engaged in unethical conduct in holding the press conference. The trial court dismissed Busch's charges and the trial proceeded. Busch now counter attacked with a new and novel tactic. The distributor who had taken over Maris' distributorship had recently purchased new trucks and each morning parked these new delivery vehicles outside of the jurors parking garage.

The jurors felt so strongly about the presence of the trucks that they sent the judge a question regarding the continued daily presence of the delivery trucks:

"Based on observations of the jurors – If care is taken to keep jurors from being influenced by discussions, media, etc.....then why are jurors confronted by Budweiser delivery trucks virtually every morning and evening upon leaving the parking garage? Since the condition of the trucks is a major issue in this case, we are wondering if arrangements could be made for deliveries to be made earlier or later"

The court, after reading the question, immediately cleared the courtroom of everyone except lawyers for the parties and each side's corporate representative. Upon further inquiry to the jury, each and every juror agreed that they were being confronted with the presence of the trucks and each requested that the practice be discontinued. According to the jurors' own question, the trucks were parked directly outside the juror parking garage. Plaintiff and plaintiff's counsel also noticed a Budweiser truck was always parked near the courthouse every morning no matter what time the attorneys arrived at court whether 8:00 a.m., or 8:55 a.m. This went on for weeks without change until the jury question. After the jury question, the Budweiser trucks were no longer conspicuously parked each morning near the courthouse.

As the case developed, it became readily apparent that the company's motives for terminating the Maris distributorship agreement were little more than a ploy based on selfishness and greed. Once the termination was completed, a majority of the Maris family's territory was transferred to the best friend of August Busch III, who then was chairman of the company's board of directors. He, in turn, transferred part of those territories to the chairman's brother. In short, the termination of one of one of America's most successful beer distributorships was designed solely to further enrich Busch family members and friends. Under Maris management, the territories had seen sales increase from $3 million in 1968 to over $50 million in 1996.

Perhaps because the company's motives were so closely related to the Busch family interests, the defense attorneys pulled out all the stops. They even stooped to hiring detectives to follow and monitor our team lawyers during the trial, sorting through trash and following them from the time they awoke until they went to bed. I learned of these efforts from two sources. The trial team was staying at the Embassy Suites in Gainesville. One day the manager of the hotel came to us rather upset. She said detectives had been prowling around asking questions about us and trying to get information about our actions, who we talked to and what kind of materials we were keeping in our rooms. This was a major case, but nobody expected that Anheuser-Busch would hire investigators to follow us around and check through our garbage. I have to admit that I found it hard to believe at first, but it was true as later events confirmed.

Busch's lawyers pulled out all the legal stops of usual trial advocacy in attempts to disparage the character of the Maris family and their witnesses. A most blatant attempt was one in which they attempted to introduce evidence before the jury as to the amount of a charitable contribution shown on the distributorship's financial records. We objected to the introduction on the grounds of such evidence had no relevancy to the issues in the case and was designed only to prejudice and inflame the jury against the Maris family. Busch's lawyers persisted and a hearing on the matter was required. The following is a court transcript of the hearing:

April 18 2001, P31, L1toP36L17

PARENTI: "Thank you, your Honor, Your Honor, the next item has to do with the reference – they have a chart. They produced a chart. They propose, I believe, to argue this to the jury in opening and perhaps in voir dire, and I would like to approach the bench on that as a proposed chart relating to Mr. Maris – strike that – Maris Distributing Company's contributions. Counsel mentioned this in court yesterday suggesting to the jury an amount, which I am not going to repeat, but its here in the chart. He is going to propose to argue it to the jury. He repeated it in open court here today. In our judgment, that was absolutely uncalled for. It's highly prejudicial to make a statement like this. And he argued this in the federal case. He mentioned that to the jury in the federal case. He repeated this statement. We object to this, Your Honor. It's so prejudicial and inflammatory. We move that such evidence not be allowed."

THE COURT: "Counsel?"

MR. MOLL: "Well, it – Maris Distributing gave 60 bucks to charity in 1996. That's disgraceful is what it is. It's not prejudicial. It's disgraceful."

THE COURT: "Wait a minute, Counsel. How's it anybody's business? I mean, is it your business? Is it – how's it relevant to anything?"

MR. MOLL: "Here's the way it's relevant, Your Honor."

MR. MOLL: "In Paragraph 1 of the Equity Agreement, Maris

Distributing got an exclusive territory from Anheuser-Busch in order to invest in their business and be active in the community and to participate in the community and establish their name in the community. And one of the problems we have here is that Rudy Maris wasn't out there in the community participating, spending money, and doing the things for community involvement that he should have done. It's directly on point with the deficiencies. Secondly, Your Honor, and I'm not an accountant, but profits. You're going to hear Maris is profitable. Maris made all this money. We saw the chart yesterday, the profits going through the ceiling. How do you get profits? How do you get that? You take your revenues. I'll call them gross revenues. Again, I'm not an accountant. You take away your expenses, and you get profits.

"Now, there's one – there's two ways to drive profits up. One is you increase this number, and two is you decrease this number, and that's what they did here, invested it in the business. They didn't invest it in the community. We kept telling them, you have to pay your employees better so you can stop the turn over. It was one of the deficiencies. They didn't give them a raise for three years. We kept telling them you got to do this stuff. These expenses are relevant, and the fact that Maris Distributing wasn't active out there in the community is directly relevant to the termination, to the deficiencies, and to these ridiculous profits. Sure you can have ridiculous profits, but they can't be standing up and saying, we were the most profitable. We made profits. We made profits, and then say, but they can't talk about how we made them."

THE COURT: "You got to be kidding?"

MR. MOLL: "No, I'm not kidding. Its part of our case."

THE COURT: "Motion granted. Write this. Let me make the record abundantly clear on that last ruling. I believe the probative value of the amount of the charitable donations of Defendant Maris being $60 is the kind of evidence that the inflammatory effect on a jury outweighs the probative value on that as a relevant issue, as a relevant piece of data concerning the profits. I believe it would be such that it would only inflame the jury far beyond the value it has to shed light on the issues before the jury."

THE COURT: "Call your next matter."

The hostile and arrogant attitude by the Busch lawyers continued throughout the trial and was not lost on the jurors. Here were the big-city lawyers, beating up on the juror's hometown hero family, well known for their civic contributions. This was another defense mistake that would cost them dearly.

The "you got to be kidding" statement of Judge R.A. "Buzzy" Greene in his ruling became our favorite response to later frequent attempts by Busch's lawyers to engage in similar trial tactics. The lawyers' actions later formed the basis for the filing of a complaint against them with the Florida Bar for their trial misconduct.

The actual trial spanned three months, during which 93 witnesses testified and 610 exhibits were introduced into evidence for consideration by the jurors. In all, the trial transcripts totaled 14,000 pages. During the course of the trial, the judge separated Maris' claim against Busch for defamation. That case would be tried later.

We were confident that the liability issue would be in our favor but the amount of damages to be awarded to Maris, now that the defamation claim had been separated, became a problem to us, which later became evident in the jury's award. Gary and McClellan presented the closing argument to the jury in an eloquent and professional manner but the billion-dollar verdict was not to be.

In August of 2001, the case was submitted to the jury and a verdict of $139,698,500 in damages to Maris Distributors was returned. The verdict was reduced to $50,000,000 by the judge because of what he perceived to be an error on the jury's part.

We appealed the judge's decision. On December 2001, the appellate court agreed to accept the case as being a "final order" and thereby appealable. After the transcripts and briefs were filed and the case was ready for oral argument, the appellate court changed its mind and ruled that the defamation case would have to be tried first and a verdict rendered there, before they would consider any appeals. Another two years of time and expenses wasted.

In the interim, however, Busch and its lawyers were not resting on their oars. They prepared a fallacious complaint with the Florida Bar that alleged that Willie Gary had committed ten violations of ethics rules in his conduct in the lawsuit against Anheuser-Busch. The charges ranged from swearing in the courtroom to violating the judge's specific instructions prohibiting him from making certain remarks during his closing arguments. Gary also was accused of violating the court prohibition from public comment about the case by holding the press conference. The Florida Bar Association also asserted charges against Madison McClellan. The case against Gary and McClellan was tried before a circuit judge on January 6-7, 2004.

On February 5, 2004, the judge assigned to hear the case entered his report, dismissing the charges and rendered a scathing indictment of the Florida Bar, Busch and Busch's lawyers. The following are excerpts from his report:

> In passing, this Referee also elects to comment on the actions of the attorneys for Anheuser-Busch. Anheuser-Busch lost the trial held before Judge Green in Alachua County, Florida in 2001. It is clear to the Referee that, having lost the trial, Anheuser-Busch is now using this disciplinary process as vindication. Though this case does not come within all fours with prior cases, State v. Murrell, 74 So.2d 221, 226-227 (Fla. 1954) and Florida Bar v. Swickle, 589 So.2d901 (Fla. 1991), in which the Florida Supreme Court indicated that it is improper to have a private party, in essence, control and dictate the disciplinary proceedings, the extensive involvement of the Anheuser-Busch attorneys in this disciplinary proceeding is evident. Counsel drafted the Complaint filed, initiated the contact with The Florida Bar as to the individuals to be deposed, outlined

the areas of inquiry for depositions, undoubtedly prepared trial exhibits for the benefit of The Florida Bar and, other than presenting the case at the Trial, have been the active litigant in this case. Though the actions of Anheuser-Busch counsel most likely would not have resulted in this Court dismissing the case outright, when overlapped with the failure of THE FLORIDA BAR to meet its burden of proof and the issues with Judge Angel, it provides further support, in this Referee's mind, that this entire action must be dismissed against the Respondents.

Based upon the foregoing, it is the recommendation of the Referee that all Counts against the Respondents, WILLIE E. GARY and MADISON BYRON McCLELLAN, be dismissed with prejudice."

SUBMITTED this 5th day of February, 2004 of Ocala, Florida

BRIAN D. LAMBERT, CIRCUIT JUDGE

REFEREE

We were not idle during that period either and we counter attacked with a complaint of our own alleging trial misconduct and ethical violations on the part of Busch and its attorneys.

Since I was not named in Busch's complaint against us, we decided that I should be the one to sign the complaint against Busch and its attorneys in order to avoid the appearance of "sour grapes." I readily agreed as I felt I had an ethical responsibility to do so, never having witnessed such courtroom misbehavior in my fifty years before the Bar.

On April 1, 2003, our complaint against Busch, and its lawyers was filed with The Florida Bar. Several violations were alleged. One allegation, as an example of others more serious but for privacy concerns not outlined here reads:

INFLUENCING JURORS WITH DONATION

Two weeks before jury deliberations, Anheuser-Busch donated $20,000 to Eastside Shands, a health center designed to help underprivileged African Americans. Throughout the trial, Anheuser-Busch used racial issues to incite the jury. The donation appeared to be another attempt to improperly influence the two African Americans on the jury, one of whom had a spouse that worked at Shands.

MR. MCCLELLAN: "Your Honor, I want to provide Your Honor with a copy of a newspaper article, that I will advise the Court we did notify the other sources, pursuant to Your Honor's directive."

THE COURT: "I saw this."

MR. MCCLELLAN: "Is Your Honor aware that one of the juror's wives works there?"

THE COURT: No, sir, I was not aware of that. Let the record reflect the filing of the copy of the newspaper from July 17th reference to a Shands Eastside grant by Anheuser-Busch."

Trial Transcript, PP10889 L14 to P10890 L15. The transcript of the proceedings continues:

It is troubling that Anheuser-Busch chose to make a donation to a center designed to help underprivileged African Americans in Gainesville during a trial in Gainesville where the jury was comprised of two African Americans and at least one other minority. Mr. Moll, as lead counsel for Anheuser-Busch not only in the Maris case but in Anheuser-Busch litigation throughout Florida and the country for years, had a duty to advise his client that such a donation seeks to influence the judge and jury improperly and in violation of Rule 4-3.5, Impartiality and decorum of the tribunal.

After considering the allegations, the Third Judicial Circuit Grievance Committee filed notice of no probable cause and dismissed our complaint against Busch and its lawyers. Notwithstanding, the grievance committee took the unusual step in their "Notice of No Probable Cause and Letter of Advice" to Busch's lawyers by including thereof the following language:

However, the undersigned want to make it clear that their finding does not indicate that they condone your conduct in this matter. While your conduct in this instance did not warrant formal discipline, the undersigned believe that it was not consistent with the high standard of our profession.

The undersigned hope that this letter will make you more aware of your obligation to uphold these professional standards, and that you will adjust your conduct accordingly.

This letter of advise does not constitute a disciplinary record against you for any purpose, and its is not subject to appeal by you. The undersigned hope that, as a result of this letter of advise, you will exercise more care in the future to avoid allegations such as were made in this complaint, relating to disparagement of opposing counsel or parties, obstruction of justice, improper commentary and questions during trial.

Dated this 5th day of April, 2004

THIRD JUDICIAL CIRCUIT GRIEVANCE COMMITTEE

By: George T. Reeves, Chair

THE FLORIDA BAR

By: Donald M. Spangler, Chief Branch Discipline Counsel

Whether Busch's lawyers ever followed The Bar's advice or took stock in the admonishment issued would never be known, as we would not be dealing with them further. Busch had hired new counsel in the proceedings that were to follow, and they would conclude the pending cases.

In the mean time, we began to prepare the trial for the defamation case, which commenced in July of 2005, at the Alachua County Courthouse in Gainesville, Florida. Fortunately, most of the work had been done earlier prior to the judge separating that claim from the remaining counts. Testimony from well-known community leaders was presented to the jury that had been selected just to hear that claim. Those witnesses testified as to the excellent reputation of the Maris family and the distributorship, and how the false allegations of Busch and its representatives caused substantial damages to the company and the Maris family. Gary demanded a billion dollars as proper compensation in his closing argument.

The jury was instructed on the law relating to claims for defamation. The principal question the jury had to decide was whether Busch's allegations of "fraudulent misconduct" against Maris were true or false. If false, the jury was to assess the monetary damages caused to Maris. We were confident the jury would return a sizable verdict in our favor but the uncertainty always prevailed in our minds. The jury retired to the jury room to consider their verdict and we adjourned to the nearby restaurant for lunch.

At the same time, settlement discussions were ongoing, which is not unusual, even during jury deliberations. Both sides by then had a fairly good idea what the jury would do. Busch had retained new counsel to try the defamation case and we found them to be highly professional and much more willing to discuss settlement possibilities. I entered the restaurant and saw Gary on his cell phone as usual. He waved me over and whispered in my ear; "Bob, we just settled. Go back and tell the judge."

I returned quickly to the courthouse. I walked down the corridor to return to the judge's chambers to advise him of the settlement. Before I could say anything, the court bailiff approached me with a smile and said, "Quick, get everyone back here, Bob, the jury has just arrived at a verdict and we are ready to bring it in."

This was not a typical lawsuit ending. Everyone was now faced with a dilemma. Did we do the right thing? Was the settlement fair? What did the jury decide? What do we tell the jury? Those questions and many more raced through my mind as I entered the judge's chambers with the other lawyers.

The jury was excused later that day with the judge showering them with accolades for performing their civic duty and ordering them not to disclose what they had decided as their verdict. The amount of the settlement was to be confidential as well.

We celebrated that night with a jubilant crowd of Maris friends, family, local notables and business customers at one of the local restaurants with an adjoining party room. Music was provided as well as copious amounts of food and drink.

I learned later from an undisclosed source that the jury's proposed verdict and the settlement amounts were reasonably close. It has been often said that a good settlement is one in which neither of the parties are happy with the resolution. I don't think that was the case here.

I told Gary he would have to look to the next case for his billion-dollar verdict and that he would have to do it without me at his side at the counsel table. I was now eighty years old and desired to spend my remaining time completing the book about my World War II experiences.

That was another promise I found myself breaking a few months later when Gary called me to his office and told me about a new case that came in which he was sure would be the billion dollar dream.

After hearing him excitingly explain the claim against Motorola Corporation, I began to believe him again.

SPS vs. MOTOROLA
GPS GETS OUT OF ORBIT

The law is the only profession which records its mistakes carefully,
exactly as they occurred, and yet does not identify them as
mistakes.

ELLIOTT DUNLAP SMITH, Conference on Teaching of Law
in Liberal Arts Curriculum, November, 1954

When I mentioned to Laurie that I was considering joining Willie in a new case against Motorola Corp., she asked "What, again?" I assured her that if I undertook the case it would definitely be my last one. She said "I wasn't talking about that aspect," and she began to refresh my memory, an annoying habit of hers I have noticed recently, of an event that happened sixty years ago.

I was in law school. It was 1947 and Motorola had just produced its first television. It was popular and affordable. They sold 100,000 in the first year. We purchased one of them, our first, from our local appliance store. We enjoyed it until I began to note within weeks that the speaker was not functioning properly. It would fade in and out, cause an annoying hum and did not respond to the volume control. The dealer said I would have to contact the manufacturer, which I did. Of course, they did not respond to my repeated requests so I decided to sue them; my very first case against a giant.

I commenced the case in the city court in downtown Detroit within walking distance of the law school and had the summons served on the local Motorola distributor. My classmates were interested and excited – a real lawsuit rather than the dull antiquated cases they had been briefing.

Within days, a lawyer from a downtown silk-stocking firm called me and after downplaying my claim offered twenty-five dollars, the cost of the speaker. I demurred telling him there would be an installation charge of twenty-five dollars plus court filing fees. I made a demand of a hundred dollars. He sputtered but calmed down after I told him I was a law school student. He then offered seventy-five dollars to which I protested but would accept if I had the check in ten days. He sputtered again but agreed and the case was settled.

I gained an invaluable lesson from that very first case which would hold me in good stead during the years that would follow, and a lesson Willie Gary used in his career as well. Always ask for more than you would ever expect to win and split the difference on a counter offer.

I became the classroom hero and the student expert on corporate litigation, and settlement negotiations.

The case against Motorola presented sixty years later was the "perfect storm" case made for Willie E. Gary. It involved a claim by a small technology company against one of the largest corporations in the world, on a claim that secret GPS vehicle tracking technology was a subject of a theft by Motorola Corporation. "Lying, Cheating and Stealing," was the obvious theme and we would be practicing in a legal area where we had prior courtroom experience with the Disney case.

Stealing technological ideas from another is nothing new. The patent issued to Alexander Graham Bell in 1876 was stolen, or so it was claimed, on an idea filed with the Patent Office by a prior inventor, Elisha Gray.

Litigation over such alleged thefts became popular with the advent of technological advances and the adoption of uniform state laws protecting a person's ideas and providing civil remedies and punitive damages for their thefts.

Because lawyers were now dealing with "ideas," a concept of intangible, property, it became an area of law that was considered to be intellectual property and the lawyers who practice in that area became self-proclaimed "intellectual" lawyers. Although the ability of the lawyers who practice in that area had nothing to do with their "intellect" they routinely would hold themselves out to be intellectual lawyers, a term rejected with derision by the trial bar. Most such lawyers held engineering degrees in undergraduate school.

My undergraduate study was in engineering as well, and I had researched and filed patent applications on my own behalf and held two marine related patents. When Gary outlined the case to me a personal challenge was presented. I knew that much of the argument and facts in the case would involve mathematics and computer technology, particularly as it related to global positioning systems (GPS), which I had become familiar with through my marine and boating experiences.

So despite my earlier protestations to Gary about my involvement in the case, I accepted the challenge and found myself spending hundreds of hours on it, as I was now part of a trial team in litigation again against one the world's largest corporations. We would spend six weeks in a Ft. Lauderdale, Florida courthouse presenting our case before a judge and jury. I became convinced that there was a certain pre-destined order to my life, in war and peace. The fact that the last case in my life seemed full circle and somehow connected with the first was a phenomenon too serious to ignore.

Coincidently, the venue for the case would be in the Florida State Court at Ft. Lauderdale, just a few blocks away from where I observed, years earlier, my first glimpse of the very same courthouse. It seemed to be another lucky omen.

Gary was pleased as well, as the case would be tried where he was well known in the public and legal community for his legal successes and civic contributions. An excellent jury panel was to be anticipated. The fact that we would be spending our trial days in an upscale hotel in the social center of town, overlooking the ocean, added to our anticipation. My home was just a few miles north and most of our weekends saw me there.

Motorola's internal documents produced during the trial confirmed that the "secret" product involved had the potential of generating "billions of dollars" in revenue. That fact added to Gary's excitement.

Our client was SPS Technologies, Inc. Its principal was Juan Cantor, a young Venezuelan entrepreneur, who had commenced his business career as a manager of a company specializing in the area of security printing. Over six million checks were printed a month for various banks in Venezuela. The delivery of these checks was made via trucks to a bank's main vault.

There was no control of the trucks' whereabouts on their delivery routes and high jacking in Venezuela and other countries in South America, was becoming rather commonplace. Drivers, as well, were unreliable and frequently deliveries were late, and there was no way of accounting for the driver's actions or the whereabouts of the cargo.

Cantor was aware that GPS technology was used in the United States and throughout the world, for marine applications and aircraft as well, and began to conceive of the idea of applying the technology to motor vehicles. Venezuela's political crisis and lack of infrastructure to support the technology was the principle reason why Cantor decided to move to the United States in 1994 to continue his development and form the corporation, to be known as SPS Technologies.

Cantor hired two engineers who began designing the first tracking software and hardware prototype, using conventional analog cellular phones. Within two years, the fledgling company reached a point at which they had the first marketable version of the system, and they began an advertising campaign in international publications, and distributors were now required throughout the world. The internet was taking over worldwide communications and Cantor realized it was a means to send an unlimited amount of data, using a system that was, basically, international with no boundaries. Instead of a singular computer dialing to different vehicles to obtain their positions, they now had the availability of a single server engineered in a modular fashion to accept different types of wireless communications that would contact all vehicles, store the data and transmit the data to the clients. The company grew to twenty-three employees and obtained an order in Brazil in the amount of six million dollars. The principals had invested over four million dollars, but additional capital was required.

In 1999, the company participated in a venture capital show at Florida Atlantic University, in Boca Raton, where different types of technologies were being displayed to potential inventors. Representatives of the giant, Motorola, appeared and they expressed an interest in the technology of SPS.

This led to a series of meetings with the executives of the two companies and a joint venture was founded based upon a business plan for which billions of dollars of sales were projected, based upon our client's technology. Arthur Anderson was the third party to the venture. Motorola and Arthur Anderson were to participate by investing five million dollars each, to promote the technology. Agreements were signed and Motorola took over the operation of SPS and acquired all of SPS's technology and engineering, which was considered unique and novel, and subject to confidentiality provisions protecting SPS's rights. After two years, Motorola terminated the project, claiming they could not raise additional capital as agreed, and SPS went out of business. Shortly thereafter, Motorola began advertising, promoting and selling a product, which we claimed contained the "secrets" that were stolen from SPS's confidential and secret technology.

The case was extremely complex and technical from an engineering standpoint. It required a multitude of experts in computer and financial matters in an effort to explain our case to a jury, which we soon realized would be a most difficult effort. Lying, cheating and stealing are simple terms to explain. Motherboard, platform, modular service, megabytes is not. Keep it simple, was Gary's mantra. It's easier said than done.

After six weeks of strenuous trial, the case was submitted to the jury and it wasn't long before the jury returned with a question indicating a serious division in their arriving at a verdict. The judge instructed the jury to continue their deliberations and as time went on, we became increasingly apprehensive. After several hours, the jury returned with the message that they were unable to arrive at a verdict and the judge thereupon declared a mistrial and excused the jury.

It was a crushing defeat for us considering the time and expense that we expended and I was sure I could not go through it again.

We dejectedly adjourned to the war room in the hotel and Gary turned to me and said, "We have to get ready for the retrial, Bob. This is too big of a case to run away from and I know you are not a quitter." I told him that I was exhausted and had lost interest in the case. As Gary has done in the past, he pointed out to me that most of the work was already done, that we had gained knowledge during the trial, from whatever mistakes we made, and the second time around would be just a "piece of cake."

As bad as the trial loss was, we had suffered a personal loss as well. Before the trial commenced, Madison McClellan, our young partner, became afflicted with an aggressive cancer which led to his early death. I was considered Madison's mentor and his closest legal associate. He called me "Pops" to the delight of the office staff who used the more formal name of "Mr. P." in addressing me.

At our law offices in Stuart, Florida, Madison's office was adjacent to mine when he first came into the firm and we became very close friends. As his practice expanded, I offered him my office which had a corner view of the St. Lucie River and its own "executive" bathroom. He readily accepted and I moved into his smaller, but sufficient, offices. I had met Madison and his family early on when he first joined the firm. I was a boater, as was he, and I had his family – his parents, wife and children, cruise with me on the St. Lucie River. As time went on, he purchased his own boat and followed me on his first trip to Port Lucaya in the Bahamas with several of his college buddies. His father, Edward McClellan, was also a well-known and respected lawyer in Ocala, Florida. Hundreds of community members attended Madison's funeral. With great difficulty, I delivered a eulogy.

Gary again pointed out that we had to continue the fight as our responsibility to the client, and reminded me that there was another outstanding issue of important legal and practical significance. He said I should be there to participate in our anticipated victory when the court made its final ruling. The issue involved the application of what is called the "Rule of Sequestration," a term unknown to the lay public and misunderstood by most lawyers.

The rule requires certain witnesses to remain outside the courtroom during the testimony of testifying witnesses. The premise behind the rule is that it prevents witnesses from hearing the testimony of other witnesses, so that each person's testimony is his or her own, and is not influenced or tainted because of another witness' testimony.

The penalty for violation of the rule consists of sanctions imposed upon the violators, usually as an award for attorney fees to the injured parties. That aspect, in addition to the unique legal issues involved, continued to hold my interest in the case, as we would be considered the injured parties.

The rule is not an automatic one and must be requested by a party. It usually is invoked by the plaintiff at the very beginning of the trial. In this case, it was not invoked until the second week of the trial and ironically, and to their later dismay, it was the lawyers for Motorola that requested its application. The trial transcript reads as follows:

MR. MOSS: As to the defendant, Your Honor, we would invoke

the rule of sequestration.

THE COURT: All right the rule is invoked. Both sides are cautioned

to tell their witnesses the rule is invoked, what the rule is, what the rule means and the possible penalty for violating the rules.

On Nov.1, 2006, we requested relief from application of the rule to allow one of our experts to remain in the courtroom after another one of our experts testified. Motorola objected claiming it would violate the "spirit of the rule of sequestration." On Nov.13, it was established that Motorola had allowed one of its experts, prior to his testimony, to review the trial testimony of one of our experts. The court voiced grave concern over the violation and admonished Motorola and its counsel to never again put on tainted witnesses who had read trial testimony and specifically forbade further violation of the courts order. The transcript reads:

> THE COURT: Also I remind both sides, let's say henceforth and forever after this witness that the rule's invoked, the rule of sequestration of witnesses, that precludes any witness who's going to testify from talking to any witness that already had testified. It also specifically precludes a witness who's going to testify from reading the trial testimony of any witness who may have testified. There's no question about this, it's a violation of the rule of sequestration of the witnesses.

> MR. MOSS: And I'm the one that's going to take responsibility, because I knew this witness was looking at the testimony. And I know that - I believe I know what the law is. I've been through this before.

Notwithstanding the court's express instruction, the very next day Motorola put on its expert who had read trial transcripts of prior witnesses in direct violation of the court's order. The judge's frustration is evident from a reading of the transcript:

THE COURT: First of all, I find that his reading the trial transcript of Urbina, Lewis and Bhaskaran was a direct violation of the rule of sequestration of witnesses. So that's clear, unarguable, and I'm not going to change my mind about that.

When the trial concluded, we filed motions for sanctions against Motorola and its lawyers. On January 8, 2007, a full hearing was held and the trial judge, Leroy H. Moe, made his findings:

1)   That Motorola violated the witness sequestration rule and court orders on witness sequestration during trial;

2)   That Motorola's multiple violations of the sequestration rule and this Court's orders on witness sequestration were intentional, deliberate, blatant, willful, and contumacious, and that the violations substantially prejudiced SPS, affected the outcome of the trial, and allowed Motorola's Witnesses to tailor their trial testimony;

3)   That Motorola engaged in these violations for tactical purposes and solely for the purpose of Motorola winning at all costs;

4)   That Motorola's violations were not isolated incidents
        but a pattern of violating this Court's directives on
        witness sequestration;

5)   That there is no reasonable justification for the
        violations;
        and

6)   That Motorola, through its agents and corporate
        representatives present at trial, had sufficient
        involvement and knowledge of the violations
        to warrant the imposition of these sanctions.

At that hearing, the judge commented in his candid and colorful manner how the conduct of Motorola's lawyers affected him by stating:

"I did almost throw up when I heard the witnesses had been reading the trial testimony. I was professionally stunned at the enormity of the violation of the rule of sequestration of witnesses by attorneys that I have found to be in the past, nothing but professional, competent, full of character, integrity and knowledge...even in the highly stressful area of high-stakes litigation. So there's no doubt in this mind this was an intentional deliberate, blatant, willful and contumacious disregard of the rule of sequestration of witnesses. There's no question in my mind that it affected the outcome of the case and, therefore, was very prejudicial to the plaintiffs. But there's no question it was done for a practical purpose and solely for the purpose of winning at all costs." (R 204 - 5888)

On January 12, 2007, the court entered an order finding that SPS's counsel was entitled, as sanctions, to an award against Motorola and its lawyers, of attorney fees and costs, with the amount to be determined at a subsequent hearing. That hearing was held on April 10, 11, 13 and 19, 2007.

Both sides presented experts, experienced lawyers and judges, who testified as to the amount of fees that should be awarded to us. A retired appellate judge, one of Motorola's experts, set the tone of the hearing when he testified as follows:

Q: "And that means that when we go to C and look at the customary rate that's charged and we look at the amount of hours spent, that even after the court looks at that, the court can still award a fee higher than that?"

A: "True."

Q: "Yes, sir, but talking in terms of the 19,000 hours, when you learned that SPS' attorneys had worked 19,000 hours, you didn't believe that that was unreasonable right?"

A: "I didn't have an opinion one way or the other, quite frankly."

Q: "Now, if you look at Section A of the rule, up here, that refers to consideration of the complexity and difficulty of the case in deciding an award of attorneys' fees, right?"

A: "Yes."

Q: "And that means the more complicated and difficult the case is, the fees should be higher than for a very simple routine case, right?"

A: "Yes."

Q: "And that means that more complicated and difficult the very simple routine case, right?"

A: "Probably."

Q: "Now, you came to the conclusion and belief that this is an extremely complex case based on your review of the record, right?"

A: "I determined that it was complex litigation, yes."

Q: "And that that was a factor militating towards a higher fee?"

A.   "Correct."

Q: "I think you testified that you considered Mr. Gary to be a star, correct?"

A: "Correct."

Q: "And I think your words were that "he's a legend," isn't that right?"

A: "Correct."

Q: "And it's your opinion that Mr. Gary should be, at a minimum, at the very top of the billing scale for attorneys in South Florida, right?"

A: "That's correct."

After consideration of the evidence presented at the hearing, the court, on August 30, 2007, entered its final judgment, which in part reads as follows:

JUDGMENT

The Court enters this order and judgment for attorney's fees and costs in favor of Gary, Williams and Parenti, and against Motorola, Inc., Edward A. Moss, Shook Hardy & Bacon, LLP, Humberto Ocariz, P.A., jointly and severally, in the amount of $22,900,000 for which sum let execution issue. (R 278 - 28214)

A judgment in such a staggering amount as a sanction for violation of a rule that most lawyers consider innocuous, was unheard of in legal history and of course, Motorola filed an immediate appeal.

In the meantime, we prepared for the retrial of the principal case and began settlement discussions with new legal counsel that Motorola wisely had retained. The judge appointed a mediator to assist in those discussions and just days before the retrial was to commence, a settlement of the principal case was effected, under conditions of confidentiality of course. The settlement was reported in the Fort Lauderdale *Sun-Sentinel* as follows:

Motorola Oks settlement in trade secret suit. Now-defunct SPS Technologies Corp. has settled its $10 billion trade secret case against Motorola, the world's second – largest cell-phone maker, as for an undisclosed sum, lawyers representing SPS said Tuesday.

Motorola and the former Fort Lauderdale-based tech company represented by prominent lawyer Willie Gary settled with a retrial set to start Monday.

Still pending is an appeal of nearly $23 million in attorneys' fees that have been mounting since the case began six years ago.

"Motorola got greedy. That's what it boils down to; they no longer needed the little guy," Gary, the Stuart lawyer, said when he filed the lawsuit in Broward County Circuit Court in 2002."

We began to prepare for the upcoming oral argument on the fee judgment which, by this time, had been scheduled by the appellate court. Within days of the scheduled date, we received word from the court appointed mediator that he was calling a meeting between the attorneys and their clients to discuss a possible settlement. Considering the state of the economy and the present financial net of Motorola, I did not consider such a meeting would produce anything acceptable to us and I felt the risk of sustaining such an earth-shattering legal judgment was worth the gamble rather than accepting a modest settlement.

Nonetheless, we consented to the meeting and as is usual, initial discussions proved what I perceived and anticipated an insurmountable chasm in our positions. As the hours of negotiations passed, however, the mediator was able to convince the parties to compromise their respective positions and at a late hour, the case was settled under conditions of confidentiality.

XI

YOU CAN'T TEACH AN OLD DOG NEW TRICKS

When the One Great Scorer comes to write against your name –
He marks not that you won or lost – but how you played the game.
GRANTLAND RICE, Alumnus Football

With the settlement finalized, the opportunity to establish yet another legal milestone was lost and so the elusive verdict Willie Gary sought was gone as well, at least during my remaining years as a lawyer. Whether Gary would ever be able to achieve that pot of gold at the end of his legal rainbow remains to be seen, but if there is any courtroom lawyer in the country that has the ability, determination and desire to do it, Willie Gary will be at the forefront of the crowd.

I cannot say that the career I ended was one of pride in what we still call the profession of law. But so long as the American society continues to believe that greed and the quest for material goods is a way of American life, CEOs, politicians, lawyers, bankers, stock brokers and anyone else in the position of power, will continue to prosper.

Lawyers are a major component of the power structure in our country and their cardinal sins are not limited to CEOs and politicians. Dethroning of prominent lawyers and judges are commonplace and the sordid details of misconduct are outlined daily by the publications.

Being greedy drives not only the trial lawyer's ego but his libido as well. Few have been immune to the temptations of pursuing females, anxious to bask in the company of lime-lighting lawyers. That proclivity probably cost John Edwards the presidency and Elliot Spitzer his job as governor, just to mention two of the latest miscreants. President Bill Clinton, also a lawyer, almost lost his job as well.

The only restraint of public and professional misconduct brought out in what we have seen in this work, and in my lifetime of experience, is the maintenance and continuation of an independent jury system that provides at least, in some degree, the opportunity for the common man an assurance of a level playing field in the courtrooms of our country. Otherwise, as John Adams put it over 200 years ago, we would be "ridden like horses, fleeced like sheep, worked like cattle and fed and clothed like swine and hounds."

The cynic may well say, in light of recent events of legal, political and financial scandals, that John Adams admonishment doesn't ring true today as Americans indeed are being victimized by the very conduct he sought to avoid. The idealist will say, however, just think how bad it would have been if we did not have the vision of our forefathers in providing a system, imperfect as it may be, to protect the common man, as imperfect as he may be, against the excesses of power practiced by the giants as perfect as they claim to be.

Throughout the course of writing this book, I have often

thought of giving it up as being a meaningless task with no redeeming quality apparent in the effort involved. I sometimes wondered why I ever started it at all. As usual, a history of a person's life can frequently provide answers to his quandaries of the day.

During my early years of practice, I became acquainted with Curtis Rundell, a young reporter for a daily newspaper, who prowled the courts and reported on current trials. He worked his way through law school and on graduation, opened his law office in Royal Oak, Michigan. We became friends and referred cases to each other.

Some time after my move to Florida, Curt asked me to join him in a case against a Detroit automobile company where sexual and race discriminatory practices were claimed. It was during the conduct of that case that Curt met Willie E. Gary. At the conclusion of the case, Curt suggested we join in a project to write a book about my courtroom trial experiences with Willie. I hesitated, but he persisted and presented me with a draft outline of a proposed opening chapter. He died shortly thereafter but his idea persisted and haunted me. After completion of my first book, *A Story of Love and War*, based upon my experiences as a soldier in World War II, I decided to finish the project in which he was interested, as Curt's legacy.

In *The Giant Killers*, I attempted to offer insight into a struggling and complicated legal system and those forces at work seeking to corrupt it. Hopefully, it also demonstrated the frivolity of racial bias and animus and offers a glimmer of insight to those among us who are entering our final years, perhaps with uncertainty and the feeling of growing uneasiness.

As the story approached its end, my doubts continued as to purpose and meaning. I questioned whether anyone would be interested in reading about the rantings and ravings of a curmudgeon barrister who has witnessed the best and the worst of trial lawyers and judges, and of the legal system we euphemistically call justice in the United States of America. I struggled to find answers to the question, "What is this profession of law?" A query I have faced repeatedly over the years. Charles P. Curtis, author of *It's Your Law*, provided one answer that seemed appropriate. Born in Boston in 1891, and educated at Groton and Harvard, he was admitted to the bar in 1919. He writes:

"I have talked lovingly about the practice of the law. I have spoken unsparingly, as I would to another lawyer. It defends what we hate as well as what we most love. I don't know any other career that offers an ampler opportunity for both the enjoyment of virtue and the exercise of vice, or, if you please the exercise of virtue and the enjoyment of vice …"

The definition helps to provide an answer to a question that many wonder, "How can a lawyer defend someone who he knows to be guilty?" Every case has two sides, and for every lawyer on the wrong side, there is one on the right side. So, every case has a winner, and that is what America loves.

I felt I needed a deeper and more profound explanation and meaning to the occupation that has consumed most of my adult life and turned to Oliver Wendell Holmes, Jr. for guidance. Holmes is commonly recognized as one of the greatest justices of the U.S. Supreme Court. Holmes knew what life and law was all about having experienced the best and worst of both. After distinguishing himself at Harvard for his literary ability, he served with great gallantry in the Civil War, being wounded three times and miraculously surviving. After he mustered out in July, 1864, Holmes prepared for the bar in spite of the gloomy warnings of his famous father, that a lawyer could not become a great man. He became successively a member of the Harvard law faculty, the Supreme Court of Massachusetts and in 1902, of the highest tribunal in the land. When Holmes retired in 1932, he had built a great reputation for the character of his opinions.

Holmes served on the court until January 12, 1932, when his brethren on the court citing his advanced age, suggested that the time had come for him to step down. By that time, at ninety years of age, he was the oldest justice to serve in the court's history. Three years later, he died and was buried in Arlington National Cemetery.

Holmes, in his last years, was said to have exhibited a trait not uncommon among lawyers. While walking down Pennsylvania Avenue with a friend, a pretty girl passed. Holmes turned to look after her. Having done so, he sighed and said to his friend, "Ah, George, what wouldn't I give to be seventy-five again."

In his will, Holmes left his residuary estate to the United States government. He had earlier said that, "taxes are the price we pay for a civilized society." One must wonder with the present carnage existing on the streets of America whether he would dissent from that opinion if asked today. Will Rogers, American humorist (1879-1935), said of Holmes's bequest:

"Wasn't that a remarkable will that Oliver Wendell Holmes left? Imagine a man giving his money to the government at a time when 120 million people are trying to get it away from the government or trying to keep from paying 'em even what we owe them.

At least eighty years of service to his country and he accumulates some money, and is so appreciative of what his country has done for him that he wants to return it. All we hear is 'What's the matter with this country?' 'What's the matter with the world?' There ain't but one word wrong with every one of us in the world, and that's selfishness."

In 1886, Holmes presented a talk to the student body at Harvard on "The Profession of the Law." The following was its ending:

"And now, perhaps, I ought to have done. But I know that some spirit of fire will feel that his main question has not been answered. He will ask, What is all this to my soul? You do not bid me sell my birthright for a mess of pottage; what have you said to show that I can reach my own spiritual possibilities through such a door as this? How can the laborious study of a dry and technical system, the greedy watch for clients and practice of shopkeepers' arts, the mannerless conflicts over often sordid interests, make out a life? Gentlemen, I admit at once that these questions are not futile, that they may prove unanswerable, that they have often seemed to me unanswerable. And yet I believe there is an answer.

But do not think I am pointing you to flowery paths and beds of roses, - to a place where brilliant results attend your work, which shall be at once easy and new. No result is easy which is worth having.

No man has earned the right to intellectual ambition until he has learned to lay his course by a star which he has never seen, - to dig by the divining rod for springs which he may never reach. In saying this, I point to that which will make your study heroic. For I say to you in all sadness of conviction, that to think great thoughts you must be heroes as well as idealists.

Only when you have worked alone, - when you have felt around you a black gulf of solitude more isolating than that which surrounds the dying man, and in hope and in despair have trusted to your own unshaken will, - then only will you have achieved. Thus only can you gain the secret isolated joy of the thinker, who knows that, a hundred years after he is dead and forgotten, men who never heard of him will be moving to the measure of his thoughts, - the subtile rapture of a postponed power, which the world knows not because it has no external trappings, but which to his prophetic vision is more real than that which commands an army. And if this joy should not be yours, still it is only thus that you can know that you have done what it lay in you to do, - can say that you have lived, and be ready for the end."

Those words written by Holmes many years ago, helped me to lay the course guided by that judicial "star I have never seen," and to conclude the long journey experienced and undertaken for this work.

THE END.

TABLE OF CASES CITED

1) IN THE CIRCUIT COURT OF THE FIRST JUDICIAL DISTRICT OF HINDS COUNTY MISSISSIPPI CIVIL ACTION NO. 91-67-423

JEREMIAH J. O'KEEFE, SR., et al, Plaintiffs
Vs.
THE LOEWEN GROUP, INC., et al, Defendants

2) IN THE CIRCUIT COURT OF THE NINTH JUDICIAL CIRCUIT IN AND FOR ORANGE COUNTY, FLORIDA CASE NO. CI 97-134

ALL PRO SPORTS CAMPS, INC.,
A Florida Corporation, et al, Plaintiffs
Vs.
WALT DISNEY COMPANY, a Delaware
Corporation, et al., Defendants

DISTRICT COURT OF APPEAL OF FLORIDA,
FIFTH DISTRICT, 1999
727 So.2d 363

3) IN THE CIRCUIT COURT OF FLORIA, EIGHTH JUDICIAL CIRCUIT, IN AND FOR ALACHUA COUNTY, FLORIDA CASE NO. 97-22-CA Division 1

MARIS DISTRIBUTING CO., Plaintiff,
vs.
ANHEUSER-BUSCH, INC., Defendant

4) IN THE CIRCUIT COURT OF THE SEVENTEENTH JUDICIAL CIRCUIT IN AND FOR BROWARD COUNTY, FLORIDA Case No. 02-003159-13

SPS TECHNOLOGIES CORPORATION, A Florida Corporation, Plaintiff
Vs.
MOTOROLA, INC., Defendant

The Giant Killers

TAKING ON AMERICA'S LARGEST CORPORATIONS

Robert V. Parenti

Robert V. Parenti has been a trial attorney for more than fifty years, having been admitted to the Michigan Bar in 1951, after his military service.

The last twenty years of his practice has been in Stuart, Florida where he now resides, finally retired, with his wife Laurie.